PR

Assessment

M000187886

"This book links two critical topics in education today: the use of educational technology and the need for meaningful assessment. The author provides a treasuretrove of activities and examples to enhance teaching and learning. Ms. Meldrum aptly demonstrates not only how the use of technology in the context of assessment can be achieved but also makes a compelling argument that technology is a driver towards equity. This book celebrates the convergence of the potential of technology and the need for differentiation in education. A must-read for today's teacher!"

—**Cindy Finn**, Ph.D.

"I have had the pleasure of working with Ms. Meldrum for the past few years. I am so pleased that Kim's expertise in transforming a school staff is now available to all administrators and educators. This book provides the reader with practical examples of how to use technology as a tool for learning and clearly explains the rich assessment information that can be taken from student creations. It is the first book about assessment that I can honestly say provides the reader with a clear understanding of the critical role that ongoing assessment has on student success. Ms. Meldrum gives us practical examples of how to successfully change our teaching and our assessment practices."

—**Bernadette Reichert**, Principal

"I've read many books on technology and probably more on assessment. I can honestly say that I've never read one that captures the essence of both topics more expertly and succinctly than Kim's book."

—**Sam Bruzzese**, retired Principal and Faculty Lecturer

"As a continued supporter of meaningful learning, embracing opportunity, and promoting the use of technology in the classroom, I could not have enjoyed Ms. Meldrum's book more. She truly understands differentiated instruction, while allowing students to take creative liberties with their work. She uses that framework to suggest new and innovative ways of blending learning and technology—pushing students to demonstrate their learning and using technology as an empowering tool. The landscape of teaching and assessment practices continues to change, and Ms. Meldrum's book will help any educator navigate this exciting and influential time."

—**Michael Chechile**, Director General of the Lester B. School Board

"This book is the antidote to America's burden of standardized teaching. Kim captures the true foundation of what authentic assessment should be like and provides the reader with practical experiences and examples that teachers can use in their classroom tomorrow. Learn how to move past 'data' to understand real assessment and personalized learning."

—**Tanya Avrith**, Pedagogical Consultant, Apple Distinguished Educator, Google for Education Certified Innovator

"A worthwhile read for educators across all facets of learning. This book should be required reading for all students in teacher-preparation programs as well as future curriculum and instruction specialists. The whole concept of assessment has far too long been along one very limited stream of information. This book highlights all the different elements to assessment as well shows a purposeful and meaningful way to integrate technology for the purpose of assessment."

—**Ken Shelton**, Keynote Speaker, Apple Distinguished Educator, Google Certified Innovator

Assessment
That Matters

Using Technology to
Personalize Learning

Kim Meldrum, M.Ed.

Published by EdTechTeam Press

Library of Congress Number: 2016943597
Paperback ISBN: 978-1-945167-02-7
eBook ISBN: 978-1-945167-03-4

Irvine, California

Contents

Preface

As I enter the twilight of my teaching career, I am amazed at how much teaching and learning has evolved over the past ten years. Educators have gone from standing in front of the class delivering content to students, to serving as learning facilitators. Instead of everyone using the same textbook and doing the same thing at the same time, educators now create teaching and learning activities designed to meet the individual needs and learning styles of each student. The information educators have at their fingertips about how children learn is outstanding. Additionally, we can draw on our colleagues' knowledge and experience, educational research, and technology innovation. (Our students are often more technologically advanced than we are.) There is so much that we can see, do, and learn. It is an amazing time to be an educator!

Who would have thought we would be integrating technology into our lives and the lives of our students to the extent we have? I never would have imagined I would be blogging and have an educational Twitter account. Even at the end of my teaching career, I am learning about Google Drive, Google Apps for Education, digital citizenship, and so many other engaging and exciting approaches to teaching and learning. I am thrilled by the fact that our students have opportunities to learn using so many different tools and strategies, as well as the ability to share their learning in a myriad of ways.

Digital Citizenship

Over the past few years, I have designed and delivered numerous professional learning workshops for educators and administrators about how to use technology as a tool for learning.

Specifically, we've looked at how to innovate our teaching practices so they are aligned with the world of today and the skills and knowledge that our students need to become successful adults. Consistently during these workshops, though, we hit a bump in the road that resulted in us having discussions around the following question:

> *How do I have time to innovate when I have a curriculum to follow and exams to give? Let's be realistic—I have to give my students a mark!*

The ensuing discussions from this "bump" are the impetus behind this book. As educators, we need to continue to develop our skills and knowledge in the areas of assessment and evaluation. Our students can demonstrate their knowledge in many different and creative ways, so we must develop our abilities to reflect on those demonstrations and gather from them assessment and evaluation information. My contention is that Google Apps for Education (GAfE) and the use of technology as a tool for learning can provide educators with a wealth of rich assessment and evaluation information.

I hope the information in this book will encourage you to reflect on your teaching practices, take risks, and try at least one of the strategies suggested. I truly believe that you will find using technology as a tool for learning will make your teaching more engaging, more rewarding, and less time-consuming than traditional teaching methods. Most importantly, you will learn a great deal about your students, as well as collect rich evidence of student learning to share with parents.

Technology is a tool which engages students, opens their world to endless learning and possibilities, and provides them with opportunities to demonstrate their learning in ways which are both rewarding and enriching.

Let's embrace these opportunities and give our students the skills and knowledge they deserve—skills and knowledge which will make them caring, successful contributors to our ever-evolving world. Let's embrace technology and all it has to offer.

Technology is a tool which engages students, opens their world to endless learning and possibilities, and provides them with opportunities to demonstrate their learning in ways which are both rewarding and enriching.

Introduction

As a teacher, administrator, and consultant, I have spent countless hours reading about, talking about, and exploring the many aspects of assessment and evaluation. I never felt comfortable assigning marks to students even though I knew it was part of an educator's responsibilities. Realistically, what is the difference between a seventy-eight and an eighty? Fortunately, the assigning of grades (evaluation) is only a small part of our responsibilities as educators. Our main role is to teach our students—to provide them with teaching and learning opportunities designed and developed based on their current knowledge and skills. As educators, we need to understand the distinction between assessment and evaluation. Although there is a great need to continue to develop our skills in both assessment and evaluation our main focus should be on assessment *for* and *of* learning.

To understand how to develop teaching and learning opportunities that meet the individual interests and skills of our students, it is important to understand that assessment and evaluation are not synonymous. Assessment is an ongoing process, and its role is to improve student learning. Assessment provides students with encouragement, feedback, and direct instruction that helps them build their understanding, motivates them to continue to develop their creations, and sparks a desire to learn.

Evaluation is final and provides a quantitative value to the work produced. Assigning marks is not an exact science; subjectivity is always present. However, what is critical is that we continually work towards lessening the potential negative impact that subjectivity can have on students. We need to ensure our students have opportunities to demonstrate their learning in different ways, using a variety of means and mediums, so that their creations have importance beyond the classroom walls. Since evaluation is summative, students often look at their mark and move on to the next assigned task. Real learning does not occur with evaluation to the extent that it can through assessment. By transforming our assessment skills using technology as a tool, our students will have greater opportunities to transform their learning and to become lifelong learners!

Technology can and should play a significant role in the development of lifelong learners. Allowing your students to demonstrate their learning through technology will give it relevance, an authentic audience, and longevity. Technology as a tool *for* learning has the power to transform our students' demonstrations of learning and, in so doing, can transform how we assess student knowledge. When used appropriately, not as digitized worksheets, student creations using technology provide us with rich evidence of student learning.

Dr. Tim Clark recently wrote a blog post about the differences between digitized learning and digital learning. It got me thinking about how important it is to fully understand these differences and prompted me to create a new workshop for educators entitled "Creating Teaching and Learning Opportunities Using Technology." I used Dr. Clark's blog as a starting point. I provided the participants with this example of digitized learning: An educator takes a worksheet and uploads it to a Google Doc and then shares the "sheet" with her students. We discussed that the only benefit of this activity is that the students answer the questions on the computer rather than on paper. The function of this change is simply saving paper. Conversely, we looked at a digital teaching and learning opportunity: Ask the

Dr. Tim Clark's
Blog

students to create a screencast[1] to explain how they solved a science experiment and then publish the screencast to their blog and YouTube channel. It allows them to demonstrate their learning using a different medium. This also allows students to receive feedback from a wide audience. (For steps on how to screencast see Appendix 2.)

We took this discussion further by examining the SAMR model created by Dr. Ruben R. Puentedura. The SAMR model demonstrates how technology can be implemented to transform and enhance learning. As a group, we discussed how the pyramid shape often used to depict the SAMR model is sometimes perceived as a hierarchy; you must work your way up without fluctuating from one level to another. To avoid this misunderstanding of the purpose of the SAMR model, I suggested a slight modification to the layout:

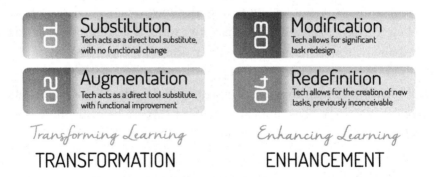

SAMR

01 Substitution
Tech acts as a direct tool substitute, with no functional change

03 Modification
Tech allows for significant task redesign

02 Augmentation
Tech acts as a direct tool substitute, with functional improvement

04 Redefinition
Tech allows for the creation of new tasks, previously inconceivable

Transforming Learning
TRANSFORMATION

Enhancing Learning
ENHANCEMENT

Adapted from Ruben R. Puentedura, Ph.D. SAMR Model   @ meldrumkim

This reconfiguration reveals the SAMR model's fluidity but what is important is that you are able to recognize which aspect of the SAMR model you are implementing. Sometimes you and your students will be at the level of modification; at other times you will be

---

1 Screencasting is a video screen capture that includes audio narration.

doing substitution. An example of substitution is taking the content from a textbook and turning it into a slide show that your students view on a screen rather than in their textbooks. Substitution does not add any functional change to the learning situation and will not provide you with rich assessment information. Owing to

SAMR Model

the limitations of substitution, the only thing that has changed is the means by which students are accessing information. It is important that as an educator you reflect on how often you are using substitution.

On the other hand, augmentation allows for subtle functional changes. A functional change would be to have your students hand in their assignments through a tool such as Dropbox. This changes your workflow because you have all their assignments in one digital location. However, this does not change the way in which they created their work and, most importantly, does not impact student learning.

Modification and redefinition both allow students to demonstrate their learning in creative and innovative ways. If students are studying urban environments and create a city using Minecraft, this would be an example of modification. You, as the educator, could see from the students' creations whether or not they understood the components of urban design. You would also be able to assess the students' understanding throughout the creation process. Modification provides you with rich assessment information.

Redefinition is the most innovative use of technology as a tool for learning. The aim of redefinition is for the student to create previously not conceived of demonstrations of learning. An example of redefinition is Club Academia, where a group of students decided to create tutorials for one another to help them understand complex concepts in physics and math.

Club Academia

They created Club Academia so that no matter where or when they were studying, they had resources to help them. Their tutorials were created using examples that were relevant to teenagers. Redefinition provides rich assessment information.

Next, I asked the participants to work in groups to create examples of digitized teaching and learning opportunities versus digital learning opportunities. I reminded them that we needed to start with the learning goals and then determine what we were going to assess their students on. For example, if the goal for your student is to learn how to read the 'an' family of words, digitizing this goal would be creating a worksheet where a student must match a picture of a pan to the word "pan," which is uploaded to a Google Doc. Unfortunately, the digitizing of this sheet does not provide any new information about how the student is reading.

An example of a digital teaching and learning opportunity involving the SAMR model would be if you take the same learning goal and ask your students to create a Google Drawing of all the things they know are in the "an" family. You then ask your students to label their drawings. From this activity, you would be able to know which "an" family words they knew, and you would also be able to assess if they knew how to write them (modification).

Another significant aspect of the workshop was the participants' use of reflective practice. At the end of the workshop, I asked them to reflect on and share a personal critical learning which resonated with them. The following are some of those reflections: "I have been empowering students and changing how I do things in

Reflective Practice

my classroom (using technology), however today I learned that I can do more." "Most of what I am using technology for is substitution and augmentation, possibly some modification and no redefinition."

Reflective practice should be an integral part of your day, as it will help you both celebrate your successes and guide your teaching. In its simplest form, reflection means taking a few minutes each day to look back and ask yourself the following guiding questions:

- What were my positive interactions with my students?
- What evidence of learning did I witness?
- Did my students have opportunities to ask questions?
- What types of questions did they ask?
- How did I guide my students?
- Was I able to avoid giving them direct or closed answers to their questions?
- How did I provide them with different methods to demonstrate their learning?
- In what ways did I actively check for understanding?

If your answers to these questions are not all positive, then you need to review the evidence of your students' learning and think about how you can make changes and put them into practice. As an educator with a growth mindset, you will recognize that you do not have all the answers, but you can find help from colleagues and educators within your district, from blog posts, and from your professional learning network (PLN). Just as students have access to a wealth of knowledge, feedback, and support through technology, so do you as an educator.

The scenarios and examples included within the book will show you how the assessment information you gather using technology as a tool for learning can help direct your reflective practices and inform the redesign and refreshing of your teaching. In turn, this contributes to the ultimate goal of improving student learning.

We have been grappling with assessment for decades. Now we must continue to develop our skills in the use of technology as a tool for learning and understand its ability to provide us with rich assessment information. One of the *aha* moments educators frequently experience during my workshops is how much assessment information is evident through student creations.

As you read through this book, I encourage you to look at the ideas and examples with an open mind. Challenge yourself to see how these examples can be transformed to work within your teaching context. Whether you teach at an elementary or high school, are employed in a private or public school, and regardless of your subject area, you have the power to transform!

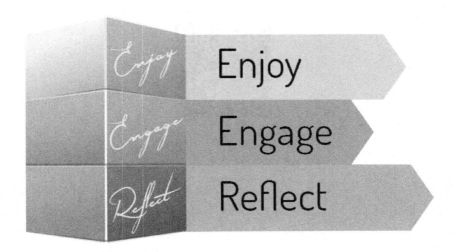

The aim of education should be to teach us rather how to think, than what to think—rather to improve our minds—so as to enable us to think for ourselves, than to load the memory with the thoughts of other men.

—*Bill Beattie*

1

What Is Assessment?

Assessment is one of the most important aspects of your job as an educator. Using rich assessment information to direct teaching and learning should be your guiding principle. Assessment is an ongoing process that informs teaching practices so that you can meet the individual learning needs of each student. When you review the students' work to see where they need some help and encouragement, you are assessing. Assessment is all about learning how students attempt a task, the skills and knowledge they have, and how they demonstrate their learning. Assessment becomes your guiding principle when you make teaching decisions based on the information you have gathered from your students. You decide the next steps to take. For example, are you going to keep teaching about two-digit multiplication, or has the student demonstrated a clear understanding of the concept? Are you going to give opportunities to expand existing skills? Assessment allows you to judge the way a student attempts a specific task in order to gain understanding. Having this information means that you are able to plan direct instruction and learning opportunities designed to build upon the student's strengths. Through assessment, you can personalize the learning of every student.

We should regularly be using three forms of assessment:

Assessment *for* learning

Assessment *as* learning

Assessment *of* learning

The graphic below summarizes these three areas. We need to remember they are not mutually exclusive; more often than not, we can use the evidence gathered from a student's creative process to inform all three areas. The discerning factor is how judgments, decisions, and actions are put in place based on the information gained to effect student learning.

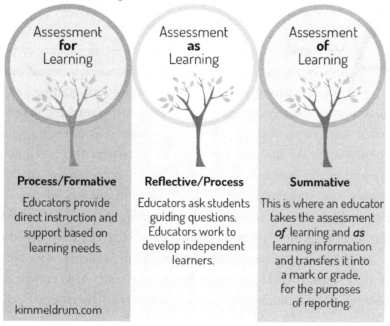

Assessment **for** Learning

Assessment **as** Learning

Assessment **of** Learning

Process/Formative

Educators provide direct instruction and support based on learning needs.

kimmeldrum.com

Reflective/Process

Educators ask students guiding questions. Educators work to develop independent learners.

Summative

This is where an educator takes the assessment *of* learning and *as* learning information and transfers it into a mark or grade, for the purposes of reporting.

Assessment *for* learning and assessment *as* learning should be our greatest focus. They guide our daily practice as we plan direct instruction and support students through guiding questions and encouraging comments. Often we hear that assessment and instruction are inseparable. This is definitely true, but we need to remember that instruction is not direct teaching only. More importantly, it is about creating learning opportunities for students that allow them to creatively demonstrate their skills and knowledge.

An example of assessment *for* learning that is common practice would be when students write a narrative and you sit with them individually to do a writing conference. You read over each student's narrative together and provide encouragement. You also make suggestions on how to improve their writing. In assessment *as* learning, you ask the student guiding questions within the writing conference, which encourages improvement, without you telling them exactly how to improve their writing. For example: *I really like the way your main character is so adventurous. I wonder what she is going to do next?* In assessment *as* learning, you are encouraging students to develop their skills without being dependent upon you.

Assessment *of* learning is summative and evaluative and really should take the least amount of an educator's time. This is because it happens at the end of student learning, at the end of the creation. Assessment *of* learning is when we make a final judgment on a student's work, herein referred to as evaluation, distinct from assessment. Typically, we provide students with a mark and, in certain cases, some comments that we hope are helpful. This is when our assessment becomes evaluative. The challenge with focusing too much time and attention on assessment *of* learning is that we are not helping the students during the process of learning. Too often when evaluations are returned, students look at their marks and then put aside their work. They do not reflect on the comments that have been added because they see their work as done, finished; now it is time to move on to the next assignment. Assessment is not the same as evaluation, so the main focus as you continue reading will be on assessment *for* and *as* learning. You will notice the careful selection of the two words throughout the book.

John Hattie, in his book *Visible Learning for Teachers: Maximizing Impact on Learning*, emphasizes the importance of educators seeing student learning through student eyes. By doing this, educators are able to gather assessment *for* and assessment *as* learning information. Too often

Visible Learning

traditional teaching methods have not provided this opportunity, leaving students without a powerful way to share their thinking processes. Worksheets and tests, like the racks of workbooks for children I saw recently in a bookstore, created in the one-size-fits-all model, do not allow students to demonstrate their individual learning processes. Typically, worksheets and paper-and-pencil tests ask each student the same question in the same way. They require that each student respond using only one method. If the test is multiple choice, then the student must circle the one correct answer; this requires memory skills or, in some cases, guessing skills. If the test allows for the students to write their response to the question, then the success is dependent upon their written language skills, not just the knowledge needed to correctly answer the question. Consequently, with paper and pencil tests, a student who has good knowledge of the content but poor written language may not get a good mark. Owing to their limited design aspects, worksheets and tests do not allow students to demonstrate rich evidence of learning, which results in limited assessment information. Additionally, using these methods does not allow students to make their thinking visible. There are students who have incredible knowledge to share, but they are excluded from the learning process because they are required to demonstrate their knowledge according to traditional evaluation approaches.

Below is an example of a rubric and a worksheet that a grade two student received.

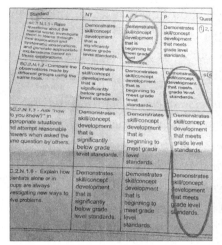
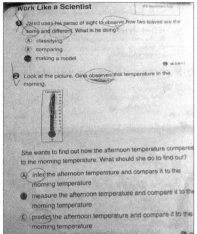

When this worksheet was returned to the second-grade student who completed it, her parents asked the teacher if the corrected paper was a follow-up to hands-on activities. The teacher responded that it was simply science work, and she sent home the rubric to explain the curriculum outcome assessed. While *observe, infer,* and *predict* are all valuable skills, they cannot be demonstrated on a piece of paper without exploring the activity with real materials. If the student had completed an exploration activity, the experimentation process could have been photographed and then uploaded to an app such as Explain Everything. The student would then be able to record themselves explaining how they solved the experiment. This would provide the teacher with assessment *for* and *of* information, making a test redundant.

You can see from the examples above that although delivering content through textbooks and worksheets may make planning easier, it does not meet the needs of all students. Marking all of those papers can be incredibly time consuming for educators and, in reality, they do not provide much benefit to student learning. To create teaching and learning opportunities that meet the needs of each student, it is imperative that educators know what skills and knowledge their students already possess. It is also critical to know how they learn. This means we must look beyond tests and paper and pencil tasks and continually review, refresh, and revitalize our skills and knowledge of assessment—resulting in substantive, important changes to our practices.

Growing Success

The use of assessment to improve student learning and to help students become independent learners requires educators and students to acknowledge and enact a fundamental shift in how they perceive their roles in the learning process. In a traditional assessment paradigm, the teacher is perceived as the active agent in the process, determining goals and criteria for successful achievement, delivering instruction, and evaluating student achievement at the end of a period of learning.

—*Growing Success*

Typically, educators employ a number of means to allow students to share their learning. At times, students are asked to reflect on their learning, which is an invaluable skill. However, asking students to reflect by "inking their thinking" using paper and pencil only works for those who have strong skills in retell *and* in written language. As previously mentioned, using this method alone to make thinking visible has excluded all other students who have powerful reflections about their learning and have great retell skills but do not have strong writing skills, so now let's examine how we might change our practices to reflect the needs of all students.

Imagine a grade three student who is given a narrative to read and then asked to respond to a number of open-ended questions. The questions are designed to assess comprehension and the student's ability to make connections. Now imagine that your student has strong reading skills, but weak writing skills. When you assess his or her written responses, are you inadvertently simply assessing the writing? Is the comprehension negatively affected by challenges the student has with writing? Had they been able to record their responses using any suitable medium, would you have a more accurate understanding of their comprehension? I say yes—for sure. Fortunately, we now have access to technology that, when used appropriately, can provide strategies for differentiation and be used to gain assessment information through student creations instead of traditional means. The power of technology as a tool for learning is an amazing way to move from the traditional methods we have just discussed.

Technology allows students to create videos to demonstrate their knowledge: to use voice-to-text to "ink their thinking" rather than being stymied by their challenges with written language; to use screencasting[1] to explain their learning process and so much more. A grade one student I was working with recently explained, using a screencast, how he had solved some simple addition problems. This short video allowed him to orally demonstrate his understanding of addition by sharing his video on his school's Twitter and YouTube channel. It gave his learning authenticity; it provided evidence that he understood the concept of addition, evidence of his oral language skills, and knowledge of the specific math language necessary to explain his understanding of the addition problems.

In his recent bestselling book, *Show Your Work*, Austin Kleon writes about the importance of sharing your creations with the universe so they can be seen by all and the powerful impact this can have on a student's future:

Austin Kleon

---

1 Screencasting is a video screen capture that includes audio narration, such as Snagit and Screencastify.

Imagine if your next boss didn't have to read your resume because they already read your blog. Imagine being a student and getting your first gig based on a school project you posted online. Imagine losing your job but having a social network of people familiar with your work and ready to help you find a new one. Imagine turning a side project or a hobby into your profession because you had a following that could support you.

Tools of technology such as screencasting, voice-to-text, video creation, blogging, and social media will allow students to share their knowledge and learning in ways previously inconceivable. Students must have opportunities to demonstrate their learning and make their thinking visible in order for educators to gather rich assessment information.

My colleague James Petersen acquired his last two jobs because of his digital identity through his blog, online presence, and online contributions! In order for Generation Z to have these same incredible opportunities, educators must create teaching and learning opportunities that embrace technology as a tool for learning.

James Petersen

The teacher is no longer the "sage on the stage" who spends an inordinate amount of time standing and delivering content from the front of the class, hoping students are receiving and memorizing the information. Additionally, simply using a piece of equipment or an element of technology isn't necessarily an appropriate use of technology as a tool for learning. For example, putting content into a slide presentation and playing it for the students is still standing and delivering. The only thing that has slightly changed is the medium.

Another teaching practice educators often mistake as being innovative is using an interactive whiteboard to display textbook content while talking to students. This often does not meet the learning styles of most students. It is a skill to be able to read off of a screen, listen to a lecture, and synthesize information. This teaching style makes it virtually impossible for an educator to access assessment information about all his students.

In the new paradigm of using technology as a tool for learning, the educator takes the role of facilitator, guide, and *coach*. The educator has the role of asking guiding questions which build on the students' knowledge and challenging and encouraging them to seek answers. Through facilitation and guiding questions, the students should also have an opportunity to help one another. They should be learning and building their skills and knowledge from their peers, not just from their teachers.

An educator needs strong assessment skills to become a guide, facilitator, and coach. Educators must develop their comfort levels in embracing the necessary changes to their teaching practices. They need to celebrate what they previously did, leave some of those practices behind, and create new and innovative teaching and learning opportunities using the tools of technology! Reflection helps educators identify what to retain and what to discard. It allows them to become critical consumers of new teaching practices. Educators need to be actively engaged in reflective practice.

To gather rich learning information, we must provide students with opportunities to *create, consume, connect,* and *curate.* In upcoming chapters, I will share many examples of how technology offers diverse ways for students to demonstrate the Four Cs. As experts in your subject areas, I am confident that you will be able to personalize these strategies to meet the individual needs of your students.

Technology used effectively allows us to reach every learner where they are!

2

Transforming Learning with Educational Technology

Technology as a tool for learning has become increasingly more prevalent in our schools and should be playing a critical role in the successful learning of our students. As such, it is essential to have a clear understanding of what educational technology is. Only then can we delve into the rich assessment and evaluation information educators can gain from students' use of educational technology.

Too often discussions about educational technology revolve around hardware and tools and do not include a focus on the implementation and positive impact it can have on student learning. Effective educational technology is about *differentiation*. Educators must determine each student's level of understanding and then design teaching and learning opportunities to meet those needs, which in turn will ensure every student's growth and passion for learning. Technology provides the way to achieve this. By using technology as a tool, educators gain rich assessment information through the creative and divergent ways students demonstrate their learning.

The role of educators is critical in the implementation of technology as a tool for learning. In its first standard, The International Society for Technology in Education (ISTE) highlights the critical role educators play in the definition and implementation of educational technology:

Teachers use their knowledge of subject matter, teaching and learning, and technology to facilitate experiences that advance student learning, creativity, and innovation in both face-to-face and virtual environments.[1]

ISTE

As I've mentioned, I am in the last decade of my career in education, but I am excited and revitalized because of the power technology has to make real change for students. My friends in education say I am a "die-hard pedagogue" because I am passionate about doing what is best for students. My teaching career started out in the late 1980s in a one-room schoolhouse where I had nine students: one non-reader in grade two, four grade four students, three grade five students, and one very challenging grade six student. As you can imagine, I learned about the need to differentiate and plan creative teaching and learning opportunities early in my career out of sheer necessity. As I wrote this book, I remembered that particular year was when I took a technology course all about Logo, an early educational programming language that I was introduced to in 1985! I was able to program

Logo

---

1 The ISTE Standards have recently been revised to reflect the ever-evolving growth of educational technology. They are currently in BETA.

words onto a small green monitor by using a robot called a turtle. I taught my nonreader how to read using Logo and a basic computer; that was innovative in those days!

I have wonderful memories of my grade five and six classes in another school. Our class had a vermicomposter, eco-jars, and a rabbit. I remember how incredibly rewarding it was to pilot conference reporting with my grade five students. Conference reporting involved me sitting with the students' parents, and for each student we collaboratively wrote their anecdotal report card. I still remember having goose bumps because it was so moving to hear each student articulate their learning.

My career has taken a winding path. I have been an educator, a pedagogical consultant, an administrator, a technology innovation consultant, and have even worked with teachers in an isolated village in the north of South Africa. I have had amazing experiences and have met incredible educators; however, I have been discouraged because I have seen how slow educational reform is—until now! I now see the huge potential technology as a tool for learning has for accelerated, widespread educational reform.

There is still a need for change in our schools, but I am encouraged by all the possibilities. I was recently in a school where I saw a stack of copies featuring a Christmas tree outline. Why an outline? Even if the teacher is most comfortable using paper, why not ask students to draw their own tree and decorate it? This would give students an opportunity to be more creative and would provide the teacher a little assessment *for* learning information.

This is just one example of the one-size-fits-all teaching I continue to see—too many isolated spelling tests, worksheets, and the same thematic units done year after year. I see disengaged students sitting in classrooms as teachers deliver content which students are required to memorize.

Using technology as a tool for learning involves moving away from the photocopy machine and moving towards tools such as Google Draw or Doodle Cast where students can design and decorate their own Christmas trees. Or you could take this one step further and ask students to create an oral story to accompany their drawing—a story easily recorded using a screencasting app.

By screencasting their story, they have a digital record of their creation that demonstrates their creativity and their oral language. Students are then able to share their work easily beyond the classroom. They have evidence to curate in their digital portfolio, and the teacher has rich assessment information!

If you are using iPads, these same rich learning demonstrations can be created using apps such as Explain Everything, Book Creator, or for younger students, Doodle Cast. Remember, the specific app is irrelevant. Rather, it is the *creating*, *sharing*, and *connecting* facilitated by the tool that is important for the student to experience.

I recently asked Ken Shelton, a passionate and dedicated advocate of transforming learning, what technology as a tool for learning meant to him. His succinct response provides a powerful visual image:

> *Technology as a tool for learning to me is similar to a hammer as a tool for building. Technology as an isolated entity cannot and does not automatically mean learning occurs. Similarly, a hammer as an isolated entity does not automatically mean something is being built. However, when used appropriately, effectively, and within the right context, technology can enable the construction of amazing learning opportunities and outcomes.*

Ken Shelton

His quote made me think of the hammer sitting in my workroom. While I use it once in a while, I do not have the skills and knowledge to create amazing things with it. This spring I want to make a raised garden. To achieve my goal, I am not going to learn more about the hammer (tool), but I am going to research how to build a raised garden bed. Gathering information will inevitably involve some online research, watching YouTube videos, and consulting with my "construction" PLN. I will also need to ask a friend with construction experience to assess my progress (assessment *for* learning) and, from that assessment, advise me how to proceed.

When administrators and educators begin talking about technology as a tool for learning, it must not be a discussion about a device or an app. These decisions must always be guided by a focus on learning goals. Unfortunately, too many decisions have been made with the focus on the device, resulting in articles in newspapers about how school districts have spent hundreds of thousands of dollars and even millions on devices that are not being used in their schools to improve student learning. Sadly, the result of these articles often negates the value of technology in education, when in all probability the reasons why those devices are not used has nothing to do with the technology itself but are more likely due to some or all of the following reasons:

1. The purchasing decisions were not based on how the teachers and students would be able to use the devices to develop rich teaching and learning opportunities within the context of twenty-first century learning.

2. A long-term sustainable plan for professional development was not created and implemented. Research has shown initiatives with little or no professional development ultimately fail.

3. Initiatives are too often dependent upon a few key staff members and when they transition to other roles, the initiatives ultimately fade. There needs to be a sustainable plan that involves all stakeholders.

4. The vision of the departments of Educational Services (ESD) and Information Technology (IT) are not aligned. ESD's primary focus is typically on student learning and student success. IT's primary focus is typically on using technology in a safe and secure way. Their focus is on tools for adult workflow, not student learning.

When making decisions about technology as a tool for learning, there needs to be a consistent vision between ESD and IT of what this looks like, because it is imperative that the focus be on the skills and knowledge we want students to learn and demonstrate. We need to give students a voice and the ability to learn new knowledge and share their knowledge in a variety of ways.

We know that when planning teaching and learning opportunities, learning goals come first. It is about students having a voice, learning new knowledge, and sharing their knowledge. For example, if the learning goal was to develop students' literacy skills, here are some guiding questions:

Is the focus for students to develop their literacy skills:

- By learning to communicate orally?
- By learning how to communicate through text (print)?
- By learning how to communicate visually (multimedia)?
- By learning how to research and understand a new concept?

If any or all of these are the goals, then does the brand of device really matter? Most likely not. Rather, the focus for using technology as a tool for learning should be on how it assists the learner to demonstrate the goals.

In that case, here are some guiding questions:

- Does the student have choice in how to demonstrate his or her skills and knowledge?
- Do the tools of technology assist the student in becoming more engaged and creative?

- Do the tools give the student access to an authentic audience?
- Is the student able to receive feedback from peers and experts in different fields?
- Is the educator able to provide the student with feedback during the creation process?
- Is the student developing a digital legacy?

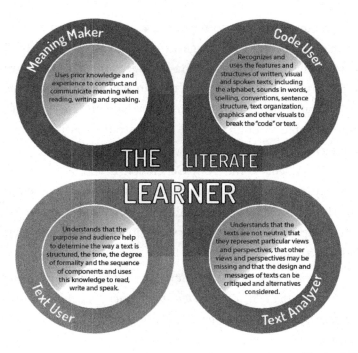

Figure 2-1

Figure 2-1 above explains how students make meaning and become literate learners. It describes qualities of the "literate learner," originally postulated in 1990 and then adapted by the Ontario Ministry of Education in 2004.[2] I believe that in 2016 with the powerful tools

2 Based on Freebody and Luke's "Four Resources Model," 1990, as cited in *Literacy for the Twenty–First Century*, Ontario Education Secretariat, 2004.

of technology now available, we must again rethink these descriptors. Students should be able to demonstrate their literacy skills through a variety of media such as videos, screencasting, website development, blogging, print media, photography, social media, etc. Students' engagement with the tools of technology should be continually reevaluated. Technology innovation provides us with new opportunities for students to demonstrate their learning. Literacy in the twenty-first century requires students to make sense of information and demonstrate their skills and knowledge through a vast range of mediums. Unfortunately, while technology has changed and provided new mediums, the processes educators use to gain meaning has remained the same. Educators urgently need to understand the assessment information available through student demonstrations using the tools of technology.

Today's students come from Generation Z and, although students have always been unique, our students today are unique in ways previously not conceived. Their unique qualities and characteristics are succinctly explained in an article by GenerationZ.com.au, an initiative by @MarkMcCrindle:

> *Contrary to what many believe, it is not that today's learners are failing the education system but rather that the education system is failing today's learners. One important factor is the way information is being communicated. On several fundamental levels, schools are often not connecting with students and their approaches to receiving knowledge. One aspect is the way many teachers communicate. In the eyes of our children, it is the teachers who speak an outdated language or teach using twentieth-century techniques ... If students don't understand the way teachers speak, then it makes sense for teachers to adopt and speak in ways that today's students can understand.*

Generation Z

In his book, *Creating Innovators: The Making of Young People Who Will Change the World*, Tony Wagner describes the skills of innovators as the Seven Revival Skills:

1. Critical thinking and problem solving
2. Collaboration across networks and leading by influence
3. Agility and adaptability
4. Initiative and entrepreneurship
5. Accessing and analyzing information
6. Effective oral and written communication
7. Curiosity and imagination

Creating Innovators

Technology as a tool for learning, used in the context of well-developed and clearly understood teaching and learning opportunities, allows students to develop the skills they need to be successful adults. In order for this transformational learning to occur, a significant amount of change within the education system is required. School districts must first acknowledge and support the use of technology in order for Generation Z to receive the best teaching and learning opportunities.

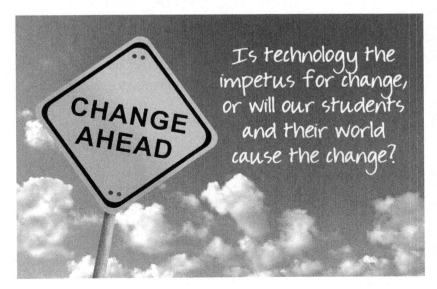

Experts in educational reform such as Michael Fullan, John Dewey, Carol Ann Tomlinson, and Grant Wiggins have collectively written numerous books and provided remarkable professional development over decades to inspire changes in teaching practices so students have greater opportunities for success. Unfortunately, change is slow. Sometimes the system of reporting dictated by many school districts puts us steadily into reverse.

Although some school districts have very well-written curricula based on solid practices, such as inquiry-based learning and constructivism, their reporting requirements are not aligned with these practices. As a result of the misalignment, educators are asked to place a numeric value on the learning of their students. Inquiry-based learning and constructivism are strong examples of assessment *for* and *of* learning because they allow students to demonstrate their knowledge through creation.

I have included quotes in this book from authors who began writing about innovating teaching as early as the 1920s. Educators have been having the same conversations for decades. Hundreds, if not thousands, of books and resources have been written about the need and rationale for educational redesign. In the context of technology as a tool for learning, the role of change is critical. While this book is not about the change process, implementing technology as a tool for learning will be a huge transformation for many educators.

Inquiry-Based
Learning

Constructivism

Michael Fullan proposed an interesting solution to the challenge of change in his recent book *Stratosphere: Integrating Technology, Pedagogy and Change Knowledge*:

> *The solution lies in the concentration of the three forces of pedagogy, technology, and change knowledge. If you want to head off destruction, **we need to make it all about learning, let technology permeate, and engage the whole system.***

Stratosphere by Michael Fullan

Although integrating technology can be a challenge, I am thrilled by the potential it holds, when used appropriately, to make learning more accessible, relevant, and engaging for all students!

3

Creating Teaching and Learning Opportunities

Our goal as educators is to plan teaching and learning opportunities using technology as a tool for learning. The greatest challenge, and unfortunately a frequent roadblock, to change is the need to develop strong skills in assessing and evaluating demonstrations of learning. Fortunately, the assessment information gathered through students demonstrating their learning using technology as a tool—combined with educators' support, encouragement, guiding questions, and direct instruction—allow us to create rich teaching and learning opportunities.

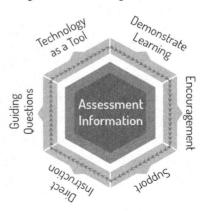

The development of teaching and learning opportunities requires a focus on both the qualities and characteristics of educators and students. Students are constantly changing and their world is constantly changing. Access to information is instant, and communication with people around the world is immediate. Students interact and gather information and knowledge very differently from the way we did; therefore, many of the approaches currently in place in our schools should not be the same as in the past.

Take a moment to reflect on these questions:

- When you want to access information, where do you most often go?

- When was the last time you read an encyclopedia—from a bookshelf?

- Can encyclopedia publishers keep content current, or is this impossible given the rapidly changing pace of world events combined with the growth and immediacy of the Internet?

- It is interesting to note Britannica discontinued the print version of its encyclopedia after publishing the 2010 edition. What does this mean if classroom subject content is taught solely from a textbook?

- How many of your daily practices have changed in the last five years?

- How many of those changes involve technology?

I encourage you to reflect on your responses to these questions in relation to your teaching practices. Are you recognizing that your teaching practices need to be refreshed? If yes, you are now actively engaged in aligning your practices with the needs of Generation Z.

The way students access information and creative tools is dramatic and should be the impetus for us to transform the teaching and learning occurring in our schools. Students must be empowered to assist us in making the necessary changes so that they will be prepared for their future! Educators will be students' guides, their questioners, their encouragers, and their supporters.

Educators will be students' guides, their questioners, their encouragers, and their supporters.

The Four Cs

A powerful way for educators to transform their teaching is by developing their understanding of the Four Cs. If you are implementing technology as a tool for learning and someone walks into your classroom, what will they see your students doing? What conversations will they hear? What will your students be creating?

In order for Generation Z to develop the skills needed to be successful, they must have expansive opportunities to demonstrate their learning. When using technology as a tool for learning, the way that these learning opportunities should be categorized are often referred to as the Four Cs. While there are a number of variations on the Four Cs, within the framework of this book we will refer to them as create, consume, connect, and curate. These Cs relate strongly to the myriad of possibilities technology offers our students.

Before beginning to improve our skills and knowledge in the area of assessment, we need to examine the role of the Four Cs in framing the application of technology. True implementation of technology in the classroom means educators need a strong understanding of the Four Cs because this is today's literacy.

The problem is not that today's learners are illiterate. They are writing more emails and sending more text messages, just in ways different than previous generations. As we have seen, they are the most educated generation in our history. The issue is that the literate forms of communication alone just won't connect in today's visual world. Today's learners are a multi-modal generation and therefore demand communication styles that engage multiple learning channels.

Generation Z
Learning Styles

The Importance of Engaging Students in the Four Cs

Why Create?

When students are able to demonstrate their learning through creation, they have a deeper level of engagement that results in learning that lasts. When students are creating, they need to think through the content so they can develop ways to express their understanding. By providing students with opportunities to create, they are able to demonstrate their learning in ways that are unique to them.

What Does "Create" Look Like?

The ability to demonstrate their learning in different ways:

- Screencasting
- Video creation
- Publishing to YouTube

- Hangouts on Air
- Animation
- Google Slides
- Google Drawings
- Blog
- Twitter

Why Consume?

Students have a wealth of information at their fingertips available twenty-four hours a day. Sometimes the information is accurate; sometimes it is not. Students need to learn how to critically evaluate what they are reading, seeing, and hearing. They need to critically reflect on the information in order to form new learning and understanding.

What Does "Consume" Look Like?

- Understanding how to effectively consume information through various media (print, film, video, etc.)
- Developing strategies to independently select materials at their reading level
- Developing strategies to use tools that aid their comprehension
- Becoming critical thinkers as they consume information online

Why Connect?

Connection is about linking students to the world by publishing their work to the web. This provides them with an authentic audience from whom they can receive meaningful feedback. As such, connecting involves one-way communication (publishing) and two-way communication (dialogue) with an authentic audience. Connecting also includes the critical element of collaboration.

What Does "Connect" Look Like?

- The ability to communicate with experts in a field that they are studying
- The ability to collaborate, to share work with other students, and to receive meaningful feedback
- Their skills, knowledge, and creation have validity, real-world relevance
- The ability to use social media as a means to share their learning with an authentic audience

Why Curate?

Curating means housing student creations together and publishing those creations so others can easily access them, such as through digital portfolios. To be digitally literate, students must be able to organize, reflect on, and revise the content they produce. Having rich opportunities to do this contributes to their development of *metacognition*, often referred to as "thinking about thinking." It is the ability to understand how personal learning occurs and how to build on the learning.

What Does "Curate" Look Like?

- The ability to group together their creations
- The ability to publish those creations so that others can easily access them (digital portfolios)
- The ability to receive feedback from others through their publications
- The ability to reflect on the feedback received and make the necessary revisions (development of metacognition)

The role of professional development in transforming learning cannot be underplayed. As mentioned previously, educators' willingness to make changes is a critical component to the successful implementation of technology in our schools. Similarly, the focus of professional development needs to change as educators' practices change. Too often conferences and professional development sessions related to educational technology revolve around devices and apps. The essential learning should not be about a device or about an app, but rather about how teachers can provide opportunities so that students can demonstrate their skills and knowledge in ways that will allow them to connect with others, to get feedback from people outside their immediate circle, to access experts, and to make their learning have relevance and purpose.[1]

In the context of learning how technology can be used appropriately in school, the discussion about apps is necessary. However, what is more important to remember is that the app should not be the motivational force. What is important is student learning. To help educators understand the role apps play in education and assist them with the selection process, my colleague James Peterson and I created the following guidelines in the table on the following pages. If you want to know what makes an app awesome or how you can ensure that your apps empower student learning within the context of the Four Cs of digital citizenship, look for the characteristics of effective apps.

---

1 See Appendix 1 for one screen of apps

Area / Description	Effective Apps	Ineffective Apps
Creation When students are the ones creating, they have deeper engagement and learning lasts longer because they are required to thoroughly think through the material to come up with ideas to express their understanding.	• Open-ended • Allow for individual learning styles • Contain simple options and rules to allow for complex student designs • Can merge various technologies (upload photos, embed audio, embed links, etc. • Make app smashing easy	• Could be replaced with non-digital media without change in function (ex: paper and pencil) • Lock creations into one app on one device
Consumption Effective consumption tools enable students to focus deeply on educational content and examine in new and engaging ways. Students have the ability to differentiate fluidly, according to their immediate needs.	• Allow for advanced search strategies • Allow for differentiation (e.g., student can self-select level of complexity) • Offer multiple input options (e.g., voice search, keyboard, stylus, etc.)	• Function solely as a PDF (no interactive or augmentative capacity) • Do not allow for selection of different reading levels

App Smashing

Area / Description	Effective Apps	Ineffective Apps
Curation To be digitally literate, students must be able to organize, reflect on, and revise the content they produce.	• Can import from other digital sources, both web and app-based • Allows students to focus on key areas • Curated artifacts are accessible outside the app	• Curated resources cannot be shared • Curated resources cannot be accessed from outside the app or device • Curation can only be done by the teacher even when student direction is age appropriate
Connection Connecting students to the outside world can be done by publishing their work to the web and providing them with an authentic audience from whom they can receive effective and meaningful feedback.	• Simple to share on various mediums such as Twitter, YouTube, and Google Drive • Artifacts are associated with a student, not a device • Student can engage with an authentic audience, which motivates and validates the student	• Creation is stuck on the app and cannot be shared and/or published • Artifacts are not associated with any particular student

Many of the examples I share in this book to encourage an understanding of what technology looks and sounds like, as well as the rich assessment information that can be gathered from it, involve the use of Google Apps for Education, (GAfE).[2] My school district and many districts throughout Canada and around the world have adopted GAfE. We have gone GAfE for a number of reasons: GAfE allows students, faculty, and staff to communicate, store files, and collaborate on documents, spreadsheets, and presentations in real time from school, work, or home. GAfE allows for students and staff to access their creations from any device anywhere in the world. If you do not have access to GAfE, many of the strategies shared can be done with other online tools or devices. Again, the device you use or the app you select does not matter, as long as it answers "yes" to the guiding statements in the table and allows students to apply the Four Cs.

In their book *Making Thinking Visible,* Ron Ritchhart, Mark Church, and Karin Morrison contextualize the need for change in our current system based on today's learners. The tools of technology allow us to make thinking visible, and the authors express how imperative this is:

Making Thinking Visible

When we make thinking visible, we get not only a window into what students understand but also how they are understanding it. Uncovering students' thinking gives us evidence of students' insights as well as their misconceptions. We need to make thinking visible because it provides us with the information we, as teachers, need to plan opportunities that will take students' learning to the next level and enable continued engagement with the ideas being explored.

2 GAfE is an integrated communication and collaboration solution hosted by Google and managed by the school district or board. The suite of tools in GAfE (Drive, Docs, Sheets, Draw, and Slides) allows students to create and share in many different ways, as will be explained in future chapters.

More often than not, our students can recommend the apps or tools to make their learning come to life. Educators need to embrace the fact that they no longer need to be purveyors of all information. Instead, they need to embrace the skills and knowledge their students have and take time to learn from them. It is an era of collaboration and trust, important qualities and characteristics of future-ready schools.

I asked Mark Wagner, CEO of EdTechTeam, what technology as a tool for learning means to him. His response says it all:

> *Technology as a tool for learning opens up many new opportunities for student agency ... for students to own their learning ... to not only be the ones creating, making, doing, sharing, and collaborating—but to also be the ones driving the learning. Asking a student, "What do you want to learn?" (and then giving them*

+MarkWagner

> *the tools and skills necessary to access and use information in a way that is meaningful to them and to others in their world) is the best way we can prepare them for their ever-changing future.*
>
> *Computers (of every kind) can also help provide a personalized one-to-one learning experience for students ... not through expensive adaptive software that aims to replace a teacher, but by putting students in the driver's seat of free and ubiquitous open-ended tools. I learned from Wayne Gretzky's autobiography that he always broke down the game of hockey into two-on-one situations ... that was where the game was won. In teaching, a thirty-on-one [ratio] is never optimal ... it's the one-on-one we have to strive for. Computers can provide many students with one-on-one experiences while the teacher actually works one-on-one with individual students who need it.*
>
> *There's no need for a teacher to be standing at the front of a class all day ... and there's no need for schools to look that*

way anymore. Technology is only one part of a modern, ever-changing school ... we also have to build capacity in Courageous Leadership, Empowered Teachers, Inspiring Spaces, Engaged Community, and most importantly, Student Agency.

To maximize the learning from making thinking visible, educators need to be experts in assessment. The following chapters will demonstrate how this can be achieved.

4

Assessment FOR Learning and Assessment AS Learning

Assessment **for** Learning

Assessment **as** Learning

Process/Formative

Educators provide direct instruction and support based on learning needs.

Reflective/Process

Educators ask students guiding questions. Educators work to develop independent learners.

kimmeldrum.com

In an earlier draft of this book, I had written separate chapters for assessment *for* learning and assessment *as* learning. However, it only seemed logical to look at them together because the creations that students make provide us with rich assessment *for* and *as* learning information. Students can spend extended amounts of time on one creation. From just one creation, you can gather incredible amounts of assessment information and learn a great deal about your students—their interests, skills, knowledge, and how they attempt new tasks and challenges.

Assessment *for* Learning

Let's start by looking at assessment *for* learning, which plays an important role in the development of lifelong learners. In assessment *for* learning, the educator works with students throughout their learning process. In this capacity, you are providing direct instruction to your students where you see a need. You are able to personalize your instruction and support for each student because you are involved with them during the creation process. Simply put, you are not evaluating their work once it has been completed. This is why assessment *for* learning is referred to as process and formative.

A good example of assessment *for* learning that you have likely been doing for years would be a writing conference. In a writing conference, you go over the student's work with them, make suggestions on how to improve or correct spelling and grammar, and guide the student with direct instruction such as, "Your character could benefit from a more detailed description."

Assessment *for* learning provides educators with an understanding of how each child learns, how they attempt a task, and the strategies they employ to gain understanding. It allows you to determine the knowledge a student has at a particular time as well as helps you to decide what the next steps are to ensure further development. Assessment *for* learning provides you with the information needed to develop your plans for direct instruction and should result in individualized planning to meet the specific needs of each student.

For many of your students, however, planning will be similar, but it is crucial that the plan allow them to demonstrate their learning in different ways. Additionally, for the 10 to 20 percent of your students who are on an individual education plan, assessment *for* learning will give them a much greater chance for success because you will have richer information about how they learn and what they know.

Assessment *as* Learning

Now let's look at assessment *as* learning. It plays a critical role in the development of independent learners because the focus is on asking students guiding questions and providing them with open-ended tasks that promote their curiosity. In the same writing conference as above, rather than directing them to improve their character description, you could guide them by asking questions such as, "I see that your story is set in Scotland. What do you like about Scotland? Wow, you know a lot. Is there a place in your story for that?" One of the goals of the education system must be to create a love of learning, and assessment *as* learning is a powerful means to accomplish this!

The significant difference between assessment *for* learning and assessment *as* learning is the role of the educator. With assessment *for* learning, your role is to plan instruction and provide teaching and learning opportunities to improve the students' skills. In assessment *as* learning, you guide students through the stages of their creation, allowing them to develop the skills needed to take charge of their own learning. While there may be times when direct instruction is needed, most often an educator's use of open-ended and guiding questions will have the greatest impact on student learning.

For example, a student who is working on developing a video about social consciousness arrives at a dilemma. She is not sure how to write a script that is both provocative but sensitive to the different beliefs of her viewers. As her teacher, your role is not to tell her your opinion and what to do; rather, you ask her guiding questions that will lead her to her own conclusion. Questions could be the following: Is there a way to inform your audience without being judgmental? I wonder if there is a role for questioning in your video?

The development of metacognition (facilitating students to become creative thinkers), is one of the primary benefits of assessment *as* learning. Providing students with opportunities to demonstrate their interests, skills, and knowledge using the tools of technology (the Four Cs) enhances their creative thinking skills. Students are encouraged to explore information in different ways and to think independently about how they would like to creatively demonstrate their learning. When students connect with others outside their immediate environment, they are able to receive feedback from an authentic audience. Based on the feedback, they can edit and adjust their creations, thereby developing metacognition. Assessment *as* learning is the means by which students become reflective practitioners!

Assessment As learning is the means by which students become reflective practitioners!

To assist their students in developing both metacognition and reflective practice, educators need to believe that students can learn independently. They need to recognize that students are inherently curious. Think about a three- or four-year-old who is constantly asking 'w' questions. "What is that?" "Why are you doing that?" "Where are we going?" Assessment *as* learning puts the educator in the role of coach and questioner and allows students to continue to develop their natural curiosity and risk taking.

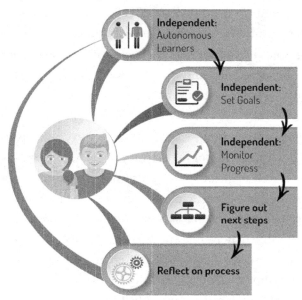

Educators engage in assessment as learning by helping all students develop their capacity to be independent, autonomous learners who are able to set individual goals, monitor their own progress, determine next steps, and reflect on their thinking and learning.

—Growing Success

In the past, educators have most often assessed *for* and *as* learning by either observing how a student attempted a task by walking around the class and taking notes, meeting with individual students, working within small groups, or giving the student a worksheet or exam. Often educators would perform assessment by looking at a student's final product. None of these approaches allow the student's work to have life beyond the class. It does not give their work authenticity.

We need to reflect on whether or not we can achieve assessment *for* and *as* learning through conventional means such as multiple-choice

Growing
Success

exams, tests, and worksheets. Can we gather rich assessment information by using content with no relevance to students and by keeping the learning within the confines of the classroom? These questions require a great deal of reflection, and if the answer is "no," which I think it is, then as educators we need to make significant shifts in our teaching practices.

The good news is that we can achieve positive change through the use of technology as a tool *for* learning. During my workshops with educators, the strategies I share can sometimes seem overwhelming, so I always remind the participants to try just one idea or one strategy, reassuring them that the benefits will be quickly visible. Change will not happen immediately, but one small change can begin the process of life-altering change for a student. Remember our main goal is to always try to improve student learning and to create lifelong learners! Now, let's take a look at how using technology as a tool *for* learning can dramatically change the information you can gather about your students.

Demonstrations of student learning, using the tools of technology, show educators they can gain rich assessment information from both the process and product of student creations. Student creations developed with technology tools do not have a shelf life. Rather, they can be referred to and reflected upon forever! In turn, this rich assessment information allows teachers to create the teaching and learning opportunities as well as the direct instruction their students need to continue to develop their skills and knowledge. They allow their students to demonstrate the Four Cs—Create, Consume, Connect, and Curate—and give learning relevance.

Accessing Prior Knowledge

As John Dewey pointed out as early as 1938, accessing prior knowledge is an important component of assessment *for* learning. The renowned education theorist wrote that new learning is built from experience. Today, the constructivist theory of education maintains the same idea: Accessing prior knowledge is necessary to facilitate real learning. Constructivists believe that new learning builds on previous knowledge and experience. The following quote from WNET Education explains constructivism further:

John Dewey

> When we encounter something new, we have to reconcile it with our previous ideas and experience, maybe changing what we believe, or maybe discarding the new information as irrelevant. In any case, we are active creators of our own knowledge. To do this, we must ask questions, explore, and assess what we know.
>
> In the classroom, the constructivist view of learning can point towards a number of different teaching practices. In the most general sense, it usually means encouraging students to use active techniques (experiments, real-world problem

WNET

solving) to create more knowledge and then to reflect on and talk about what they are doing and how their understanding is changing. The teacher makes sure she understands the students' preexisting conceptions, and guides the activity to address them and then build on them.

Since learning begins from prior knowledge and experience, educators must develop engaging strategies to access prior knowledge in order to plan for and meet the needs of individual students. Previously the KWL, typically in the form of a stencil with three columns labeled What I Know, What I Want to Know, and What I Learned, was commonly used for this purpose. While this approach was somewhat effective, technology now provides many alternative ways to access prior knowledge plus allows for differentiation and digital curation.

When looking at accessing prior knowledge and assessment *for* learning, the focus is on the educator. It becomes your responsibility to access your students' knowledge and then plan your instruction accordingly. In assessment *as* learning, the focus is greater on the student; so accessing prior knowledge now becomes a powerful strategy in assessment *as* learning because students use it to develop their skills as lifelong learners. Now let's look at some practical strategies that you and your students can begin to implement tomorrow.

 Padlet is a great tool to use to access prior knowledge. It is available online at padlet.com or as an app on the iPad. (You can also use Explain Everything on the iPad or computer).

Padlet is a great way to determine what your students already know. One way to use Padlet is during student entrance to your room. You can have a guiding question posted such as, "What do you think of when you read the words 'Ancient Greece'?" Direct them to create a Padlet where they will respond to the question. You are able to gather assessment *for* learning information about your students' knowledge within the context of the subject matter you are about to delve into.

There are a myriad of ways that Padlet can help your students demonstrate their learning:

- Padlet offers students an interactive whiteboard to use when brainstorming what they know about a certain topic or concept.

- Padlet can be used by one student or by the entire class.

- Depending on the teacher's objective, it can be used anonymously or by name.

- Using Padlet allows you to adjust your lesson planning to meet the individual needs of your students.

- Padlet can also be used at the end of a lesson. Students can share on Padlet one new thing they learned during the lesson. You will then have evidence of student learning to reflect on, which will guide your planning.

- Padlet allows the students to embed a voice recording. Those who are not strong in written language can still demonstrate their knowledge.

- It also allows students to include links to projects they have previously completed. This is rewarding to them because they can demonstrate their knowledge creatively.

Padlet

Additionally, Padlet gives a voice to students who never raise their hands or those who are never called on. Giving voice to students who are reluctant to share provides rich assessment information. Through the use of Padlet, you gain assessment *for* learning information because you are able to see the knowledge that your students already have. From

Explain
Everything

that, you can plan direct instruction and tasks that build on their prior knowledge. At the same time, the students are able to develop their skill of accessing and documenting prior knowledge. This also assists them in developing skills in reflective practice. As an added bonus, this documentation provides evidence that the students can curate in their digital portfolios. Wow! From one simple question and tool you have been able to access assessment *for* and *as* learning information!

Literacy Development

When we think about literacy development, we traditionally think of reading, writing, and arithmetic and the conventional ways students have demonstrated these skills. In order to support Generation Z learners, we need to reflect on these approaches and make some significant changes. Literacy development for today's students must be examined with a different lens because of the rapid changes in technology.

Today, students are developing skills independently through the tools of technology. For example, they are learning to complete a challenge by watching YouTube videos created by others who have attempted a similar task. Students post questions they want answered on social media sites and are crowdsourcing (using their social network either in person or online to gather information and ideas) to gain knowledge and understanding.

Generation Z students learn to read and write as children from previous generations have, but they are also learning to read and write through their independent engagement with the tools of technology.

It is critical that educators develop their ability to assess reading and writing through the creations their students make using technology. If students have opportunities to develop and demonstrate their skills and knowledge through consumption, creation, connection, and curation, educators will have a wealth of assessment *for* and *as* learning information to help them become more literate.

Early Literacy Development

Technology as a tool for learning can be used for assessment *for* learning with very young children. By documenting a child's literacy development from an early age, educators are able to assess strategies the youngster uses over time and determine if growth is developmentally appropriate.

For example, "Nina the Princess" is a video I created with a three-year-old who had strong literacy skills in place at this early age. This video also shows how easy it is to marry analog and digital creations.

Nina the Princess

Nina demonstrates on the video that she is beginning to understand the difference between numerals and letters. When I first asked her name, she told me "three," but after I spelled her name for her and asked her to spell it for me, she was able to give me the correct beginning consonant "N." Most impressive was that she was able to spell the rest of her name with random letters, demonstrating she could differentiate between numerals and letters.

After making the video, I explained to Nina's mother how impressive it was for a child of her age to be able to provide letters for the spelling of her name. I suggested Nina was ready to learn letter recognition. Over the next few months Nina's mum continued to read with her and, with the support of her seven-year-old brother, Nina worked on letter recognition, casually and within the context of reading a picture book.

When Nina was four years old, I made another video that showed she was developing word sense and knew a book had a beginning and an end. She knew that pages contain words and words consist of letters. She was able to identify the letters of the alphabet within the words, a very strong precursor to reading. She had skipped the developmental stage of learning letters in alphabetical order. I predict Nina will be reading simple pattern books by the time she enters kindergarten.

Nina at Four Years Old

If preschool and kindergarten educators create opportunities for students to be videotaped by applying similar strategies to those used with Nina, they will obtain rich information related to assessment *for* learning and assessment *as* learning. For example they would know whether or not the child had print awareness, letter recognition (sequentially or non-sequentially), and awareness that letters make words when combined. Additionally, educators will have digital documentation readily available to share with the child's parents. This digital documentation over time will reflect the child's literacy development.

Developing the Ability to Retell

Luca's Cow

Another way we can use technology as a tool to gather assessment *for* learning information is by helping develop a child's ability to retell. "Luca's Cow" is a screencast I did with a six-year-old boy. He made a drawing with Google Draw and explained his creation process. The video allowed me to assess Luca's retelling skills and identify some challenges he had with working memory. From the information gathered, I was able to design teaching and learning opportunities for him to continue to develop his narrative skills. The creation that Luca did is a very simple example of how you can use Google Draw and Screencastify to provide opportunities for your students to learn how to verbalize their process of learning. The screencast can also serve as a living example to share with his parents via email or during a parent-teacher meeting.

Steps used to create Luca's Cow

Google Draw

1. The students are asked to draw a picture of something that interests them using Google Draw.

2. Next, have them create a screencast explaining their drawing. I like Screencastify, which is available on the Chrome webstore. On an iPad, Explain Everything works very well, or choose Doodlecast for younger children. Mrs. Wideen has some excellent examples of Explain Everything on her blog. You can choose any screencasting app that you prefer because it is not about the app; rather, it's about what the app offers students.

The table below highlights some of the characteristics necessary in the development of reading and writing. As you watch the video of Luca, take note of the assessment information you could tick off based on this one short video.

What can be assessed?	Yes/No/Notes Next Steps
Does the student demonstrate an understanding of the task? What is the evidence of understanding? (What did you see the student doing and saying?)	
Is the student able to tell his story?	
Does the student express himself using appropriate pronunciation, grammar, and vocabulary?	
Does the student communicate ideas effectively?	
Is the student able to accurately retell the steps taken?	

A Google Sheet, Google Form, or an Excel spreadsheet can be used to create this checklist and observations can be digitally recorded. If done using a Google Sheet, a link to each student's creation can be inserted and shared with parents.

Another advantage of screencasting is that it helps students develop their oral language, which is a precursor to reading and writing. This is both assessment *for* learning (because you will be able to see where they need support) and assessment *as* learning (because they are articulating their learning independent of you).

Children's speaking and listening skills lead the way for their reading and writing skills, and together these language skills are the primary tools of the mind for all future learning.[1]

You can use screencasting to help students develop their skills of retell, or you can have them create an oral story using the image as their focal point. From these creations, you could assess both *for* and *as* learning. You would have information about their oral language development, their ability to retell, their imagination, and whether or not they can sequence. If the student had an opportunity to do a

1 *Oral Language and Early Literacy in Preschool*

similar creation in three or four months, you would have evidence of developmental growth, which is assessment *as* learning.

Here is an example of how one can use screencasting at the high school level. Science students can take photos of the steps necessary to complete an experiment and upload them to a Google Doc or to Google Draw. Then they can do a screencast explaining the steps of their science lab. You will be able to assess their skill at completing an experiment as well as have the additional benefit of assessing whether or not they accurately used appropriate scientific vocabulary (assessment *for* learning). Students often require direct support in procedural language and vocabulary specific to the task. By listening to their vocabulary, you can plan the support they need.

Screencasting, in this example, is also excellent for students who may understand how to complete the science experiment but have limited written language skills. It is often difficult for students with limited written language skills to provide teachers with a full understanding of what they actually know. By using screencasting, students can demonstrate their learning, and the teacher can gather rich assessment information. Quite possibly, the teacher may see the students' skills and knowledge in a very different light.

Screencasting has the potential to positively impact students' oral language skills, as mentioned previously, but warrants repetition; oral language is critical to the development of reading and writing. Without strong oral language, students are unable to understand concepts and new information. Think about what is happening as you read this book. You are hearing the words in your head, but if you are unfamiliar with a word, it significantly limits your understanding of the text. The same is true for students. Unfortunately, oral language is not a predominant focus in high school even though subject-specific courses such as geography, history, and math are rich in language. It is essential that as educators we reflect on the role of oral language so that our students' understanding of concepts is not hindered by their literacy skills.

Screencasting can play a critical dual role—providing a way for students to demonstrate their understanding and giving educators a means to gather rich assessment information. Here are several examples of how screencasting can be used to gather assessment *as* learning information.

Student Activity	Student Demonstration	Teacher Assessment as Learning
Creates a video explaining the steps of her learning	· does not speak clearly · mumbles at times · appears to have moved away from the microphone	· watches the video with the student · points out times when they do not understand the student · asks the student to find a video featuring a speaker who is very clear · asks the student to find a video featuring a speaker who is unclear · discusses the differences with the student · encourages the student to determine changes they need to make · asks student to revise the activity
	· explains the steps used to complete the task	· compliments student on her ability to explain the steps taken to complete the task
	· uses colloquial language rather than vocabulary specific to the task	· discusses with student how to develop and demonstrate vocabulary specific to the task

Student Activity	Student Demonstration	Teacher Assessment as Learning
Student edits her video	· demonstrates all desired qualities	· compliments student's success and encourages publication of the video to an authentic audience · assesses the student's skills in following editing · suggestions; assists and prompts the student through the process · shares the student's video with her classmates to assist them in their understanding of the task · encourages the student to curate the video as part of their digital portfolio

Developing Reading Fluency

Technology can also be used for assessment *as* learning for reading fluency. Matteo was in the second grade but almost a nonreader when I started working with him. After two years, he was reading at grade level; however, when his teachers assessed his reading level, he scored below grade level because of word substitution. Matteo and his parents were discouraged and confused because his teachers and I did not agree about his progress. Word substituting did not interfere with his comprehension. I realized that the teachers were counting word substitution as errors and not attending to the fact that, despite substitution errors, he derived meaning from the text.

Matteo's problem prompted me to use screencasting to show him the specific challenges he had during the reading assessments and help him learn to self-monitor when reading. Matteo used the screencast to listen to himself read as he followed along with the text so he could see where and how frequently he made word substitutions. Although the motivation to teach him to self-monitor for word substitution was based on the results of his running record, I recognized that the skills of self-monitoring would be essential for him in high school where he would experience more complex, subject-specific text.

This assessment *as* learning strategy helps students become independent learners by developing their strategies of self-correction and self-improvement. In addition, it provides the teacher with strong information about how a student attempts a reading task—assessment *for* learning.

Matteo and
Reading Fluency

Readng A-Z
Running Record

Revision History

Within Google Docs there is a powerful tool called Revision History. It is great for accessing prior knowledge and for developing literacy skills. Revision History records a student's writing history as they create and edit a document. You can access the Revision History and gain valuable insight into the student's writing process at any time. Figure 4-1 shows the steps to creating a Google Doc and then how to access Revision History.

In Figure 4-2, you can see a small sample of my Revision History as I wrote this book. You can see the number of revisions I made and the date and time of each edit. I made changes to the wording of a number of sentences and made a spelling correction and a grammar correction. From an educator's perspective, you can see that I self-corrected as I reread the document. You can also see the amount of time I

Figure 4-1

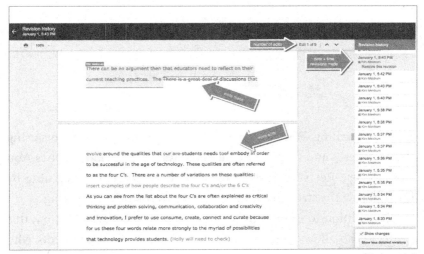

Figure 4-2

spent on my work. Through these types of observations, educators can assess the strengths and weaknesses of a student's writing and make their praise and interventions more efficacious.

Through Revision History, you are able to see if your students are having challenges maintaining the tense of their text; you could then offer them some direct instruction in that area. This would be assess-

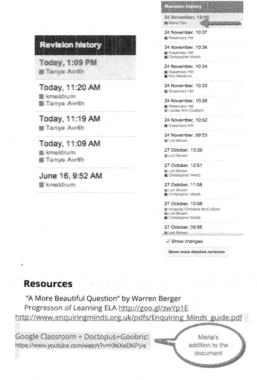

Resources

"A More Beautiful Question" by Warren Berger
Progresson of Learning ELA http://goo.gl/zwYp1E
http://www.enquiringminds.org.uk/pdfs/Enquiring_Minds_guide.pdf

Google Classroom + Doctopus+Goobric:
https://www.youtube.com/watch?v=r0NXeDKPyis

ment *for* learning. You can provide this support for your students using the comments and suggested edits tools available in Google Docs. You can also use Revision History to provide assessment *as* learning by highlighting the strengths that you see in your students' writing.

In addition to examining a single student's Revision History, this strategy also allows you to see the individual work of students who have collaborated on an assignment. In the screenshots above, you can see the Revision History done on a shared document. Each person is assigned a different color so his or her revisions can be identified easily.

Finally, you can see the contributions of each student on a shared document. This is a gift to all educators who have students collaborate on documents. Educators know that, all too often, the result of collaboration is a conversation with some students claiming to have done all of the work. Revision History eliminates arguments like, "But sir, George did not do any of the writing. I did it all." You now have evidence of each student's contribution on the Google Doc forever!

This raises an essential point: Educators assume students who collaborate on assignments have the skills necessary to work together successfully. Revision History allows you to see the contributions each student has made, assess collaborative efforts, and plan the support necessary to ensure each student is a successful contributor.

Whether you are working collaboratively or alone, think about the rich assessment information you could gain from access to not only the finished piece of writing, but also the entire writing process from start to finish! You will be able to see easily how students who are writing narratives are able to form their sentences. You will have documentation of your students' entire editing process. This information allows you to plan targeted, direct instruction with each student in the area he or she needs to develop. You can also provide your students with direct, positive reinforcement and specifically praise them for their demonstration of targeted writing skills. With assessment *for* information and Revision History, you are able to provide responsive teaching interventions and support during the process of creation, not simply at the end.

Helping Students Who Have Reading Challenges

If you want to provide the student with direct feedback, add a voice message to the document using an app such as **Kaizena**, which is available through the Chrome Web Store. This is extremely powerful for a student with reading challenges who may not understand written feedback.

How to Use Kaizena

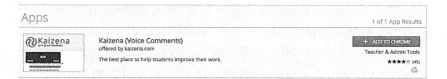

Draftback (draftback.com) is an interesting Chrome extension that teachers are starting to use to gather assessment *for* learning information. If you want to see every keystroke a writer has made on a Google Doc, install Draftback, which is also available through the Chrome Web Store.

Draftback

Once you install Draftback, a small window appears by the tool bar of the Google Doc. Simply click on the window to see the play-back—to date I have made 41,832 revisions.

By using Draftback you are able to see stroke-per-stroke how a student has attempted a written task. While using Draftback on an entire document would be tedious, playing back part of the student's writing process can provide valuable assessment *for* learning information. An added bonus is that the processes recorded by Revision History and Draftback are permanently saved for future reference. A student creation written on paper is typically evaluated as an end product with some attention given to structure, grammar, and punctuation (assessment *of* learning). Technology as a tool for learning, using the strategies above, allows for the focus to be on the process of learning and development (assessment *for* learning).

In terms of assessment *for* learning, you can gather evidence about the student's:

- strength of conventional spelling
- ability to write in complete sentences without significant editing
- fluidity in writing
- ability to self-edit for grammar
- ability to self-edit for clarity of written expression
- ability to sequence the text
- ability to self-edit sentence structure

The information gained above will provide you with the knowledge needed to plan direct instruction for your student. The support that you can provide to the student will be specifically designed for his or her individual strengths and weaknesses.

To help your students develop their writing skills, their reading skills and their ability to self-edit there is an incredible tool available through **TextHelp**. **Read and Write** works alongside a Google Doc and provides students with the tools that can be seen below.

One of the most powerful aspects of Read and Write is that it offers students the ability to have text read to them. Over the past few years I have worked with teachers and students who are reluctant writers. The use of this feature in Read and Write has given them greater confidence in expressing their

Read and Write

thoughts and creativity through text. This is because they are able to listen to their writing and edit from hearing it rather than trying to read it back to themselves. As mentioned previously reading and writing is developed from oral language.

Imagine the assessment for and as learning that you will be able to gather from your student's writing and editing process when marrying the use of Read and Write and Revision History! You will be able to see that your student has understanding of what they have been learning because they can now write it. You can see that your student has incredible creativity that previously they could not write coherently. You can go through their Revision History and see how by listening to their writing they have been able to self correct.

Read and Write offers a number of other features such as a dictionary and word prediction which greatly benefit students and will allow you to access a huge amount of assessment *for* and *as* learning information.

Another incredible technology tool for students is **voice-to-text,** now available through Google Docs as seen in the graphic below. It is also available through Read and Write, which can be used on an iPad or on a Google Doc.

Do you have a student in your class with very strong understanding of new concepts and rich general knowledge, yet who is unable to demonstrate his skills on exams because of his weak written language? Voice-to-text is a simple strategy capable of changing the academic life—and likely self-confidence—of these students!

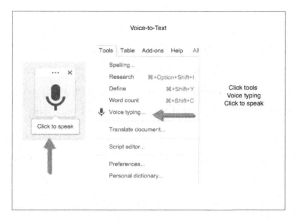

Students can demonstrate their learning using voice-to-text to create essays, projects, or simply to record their understanding of a new concept. Educators can use these demonstrations to gather information about the student's knowledge, as well as how she attempted a task, and plan further direct instruction.

When I first discovered voice typing and saw how easy it was to use, I thought about several students I had taught over the years whom I did not assess properly. The traditional assessment methods available at that time did not provide the means for these students to share their knowledge with me. I also thought about some of my peers when I was an elementary student—one of my neighbours in particular. His grade six teacher used to yell at him because he could not show his learning with paper and pencil. I know for a fact that this had a horrible effect on his self-esteem. At the age of forty, he was diagnosed with dyslexia. Imagine if he had the tools of technology that are now available. I think his adult life would have looked very differently. Voice-to-text is such a simple tool, but it can have life-altering effects!

Voice-to-text is such a simple tool, but it can have life-altering effects!

Maria Pan, a teacher from Beurling Academy in Montreal, has been involved in a one-to-one Chromebook initiative for three years. Below is her account of how using technology as a tool transformed the learning of one student and provided her with rich assessment information and new insight into the student's learning:

Tania is a very reluctant reader and writer. All previous elementary school records indicate that she is well below her reading level by at least three years. At the beginning of the year, having had no Chromebooks yet in my class, we pretty much stuck with the traditional pen-to-paper method of learning assessments. As predicted, I never really received much work from Tania. She would write very little and hardly answered questions in class. I recommended her to our Resource team so that she could receive more support.

Tania in February 2016: It has been two weeks since having received the Chromebooks, and the change in Tania's academic performance, as well as her emotional well-being, are quite startling. Tania produces work—and a lot of it! She enjoys working with a Chromebook, especially with the writing tools that she instantly has access to, namely the "Read and Write" extension. She regularly uses the "Speech Input" so that, for the first time, I am seeing what she is thinking. I no longer think that she is as weak as I originally thought. I used to think that she had a problem with basic comprehension. Moving away from the traditional methods of assessment and adopting other learning modalities have allowed me to see her thought processes. Simply put, using the tools of technology has bypassed her writing obstacles and has unlocked her thought processes that were always present, but not made visible when asked to merely write her thoughts down.

It makes me wonder how often we, as teachers, have errantly assessed our students simply because we opted for only a few traditional ways of assessment. Now with technology readily at our fingertips, it would be mispractice not to capitalize on the myriad of ways to unlock what is inside a student's mind. It's not so much that Tania "didn't know"—it was more that we, as teachers, "didn't know." We didn't know how to allow Tania to show us what she knew.

I not only see her now in a new light, but I also truly believe she is a changed student. She is more confident now in my class. Where once my classroom was a source of stress and discouragement, it is now a forum for true learning opportunities.

Voice-to-text is also a great resource for educators to use to record their observations of student learning. At the end of the day, you simply dictate your observations into a Google Doc rather than taking the time to write everything down. Additionally, you will have a quick reference of what happened during the day to use for planning.

Research and Assessment *for* and *as* Learning

For students to develop their understanding and knowledge, they need to independently select materials at their reading levels. They need to learn to use the tools of technology to aid their comprehension. Students also need to become critical thinkers as they consume information online. These skills need to be part of an educator's repertoire of assessment *for* learning and part of a student's repertoire of assessment *as* learning.

Students must learn how to access and filter through online information. For example, an Internet search often produces thousands of sites. For a reluctant reader, looking through even a small number of these sites to determine if reading them is necessary feels tedious. More often than not, the student will be overwhelmed and quit. A simple search tool that can help this student quickly identify the sites they need to read is "Command+F" on an Apple device or "Ctrl+F" on other devices. This tool enables the student to enter key text to locate key terms as well as see the frequency of the key term on the webpage. The student can then decide whether or not the site is worth reading.

In this scenario, the educator's role in assessment *as* learning is to assist the student in becoming an independent learner. The teacher shows this valuable strategy to the student and then monitors to ensure the student is using it to gain understanding. The student's creation will provide evidence of learning. If the student does not use the strategy, he will not be able to access the necessary information to complete his task without asking for assistance. The information in his creation will be inadequate or inaccurate. By using a simple search strategy, a student is able to independently develop his ability to research and to gain understanding.

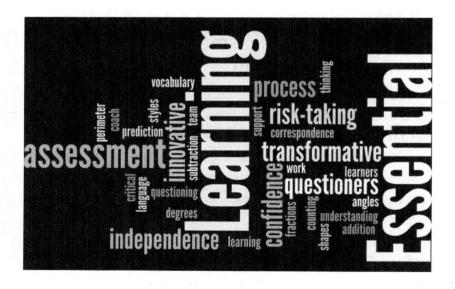

STEM

We are hearing a great deal about the role of STEM (science, technology, engineering, and math) in schools today. Giving students opportunities to learn how to code, build, and design will allow them to demonstrate an incredible amount of science, engineering, math, and oral language skills.

Recently, my colleague Antonio Fuoco and I designed an Innovation Center for an elementary school. We have been supporting the educators at Christmas Park in understanding the role that innovation and technology plays in the learning of their students. Through the use of a 3-D LEGO wall, robotics, such as Dash and Dot, LEGO Wedo, and LEGO Mindstorms, as well as tools such as Raspberry Pi, Ozobots, and Osmos, the teachers have been able to identify many skills that students can demonstrate through their creative use of all of these tools. The Wordle[2] on the previous page includes the skills that the educators saw demonstrated in a single hour of exploring the tools.

Christmas Park

In September, the students will become actively engaged in creation, so keep an eye on the Christmas Park website (christmaspark.lbpsb.qc.ca) to see how their new learning is being assessed.

Technology and Conics

Another example of using technology as assessment *for* learning is demonstrated through this screencast created by an eleventh-grade student. He was learning to design a graphic using conics and Desmos, an online graphing calculator. His teacher shared with me that he typically did not participate in class discussions and was extremely quiet and introverted. However, through his screencast, she was able to see he had

---

2 A wordle is a word cloud that uses the frequency of the same word to determine its font size.

a deep understanding of conics. She was also very pleased to be able to hear that his understanding was rich enough to explain his strategies. He had independently decided that he needed to create folders for each aspect of his design. From this evidence, his teacher was able to design new and more challenging tasks for him.

Jane Preston, Adrian's teacher, explains below how some math topics can be dry and uninspiring. Jane felt conics was one of those topics and wanted to create a project where students could explore their creative side, learn the required math concepts, and see how conics could be used in a real-life context. Jane's reflections of this assignment are compelling:

Conics Project

I had been doing a paper version of the project for a few years and then discovered Desmos. I felt this was a good way to upgrade the project. After a quick demonstration of the application and a couple of classes for students to explore it, I soon discovered the learning capacity of the students was enormous, and their knowledge of Desmos soon surpassed mine. They discovered things I did not know the app could do and started learning from one another as they shared what they were able to do.

By the end, it was clear their understanding of conics and any other equations they had used had increased tremendously. Plus, their interest was piqued and the diagrams they produced were absolutely phenomenal. Their level of achievement and interest was way beyond anything I would have predicted.

*Additionally, through observing their creations, I was able to gather both assessment **for** learning and assessment **as** learning information and, combined with a screencast, I also obtained rich assessment **of** learning information. Most powerful was seeing the students work collaboratively, assisting one another in the creative process. This was an amazing learning experience* *for the students—and for me. Plus, they now have rich pieces of evidence that demonstrate their learning and live on my YouTube channel. My only regret is not using Desmos sooner.*

Jane's reflections indicate this was a learning process for her as well as for her students. Giving her students an opportunity to demonstrate their learning through Desmos gave Jane rich assessment *for* and *of* learning information on which she could reflect.

Desmos

Technology in the Science Class

Tracy Zordan is actively engaged in using technology as a tool to create and implement teaching and learning opportunities for her students. She created a "marshmallow challenge," which not only provided rich assessment *as* learning information, but also allowed her students to collaborate, create, and curate their learning in an authentic way. (See Appendix 3 for detailed instructions on the challenge.)

Tracy used this assignment with her ninth-grade students during the first three days of school. Students were randomly divided into mixed-gender groups and assigned to build the tallest possible free-standing structure from the following materials she provided: spaghetti, tape, string, and a marshmallow—and the marshmallow had to be at the top of the structure!

Not only were there individual and collaborative elements of the project, but students also used iPads for part of the project and created their final report using Explain Everything. Technology allowed the students to document their progress during the challenge and to collaborate on their report. Since this experience was new to the students and they did not know Tracy's goals for the activity, they communicated and collaborated throughout the challenge. Students planned individually, shared their design plans with their group, evaluated them, and then designed a group consensus plan. Tracy's reflections on this activity as assessment *as* learning are noteworthy:

> *Because the students reflected on changes they would have made to the group's design and process, and shared this in their presentations, their thinking was visible. Additionally, the presentations were shared with the class, which allowed the group to analyze and give feedback about the visual aspects of their presentation—leading to a level of visual literacy awareness as well as planting the idea of a larger audience.*
>
> *I found implementing this challenge with the technology component shifted the focus to the students and allowed them to work through the learning during the activity.*

Tracy's examples and reflections validate that educators can allow students to demonstrate their learning in different ways for the purpose of summative assessment.

It is difficult to conclude this chapter because assessment *for* and *as* learning are such important parts of our role as educators, but I have decided to briefly introduce the roles of social media and digital portfolios, even though they are two books in and of themselves. You have seen through the examples in this chapter that students can share their creations through a vast range of social media sites. By sharing their creations (connect), they are able to access information from experts; they are able to gain new knowledge that is timely; and they are able to receive feedback from a host of readers. From that feedback, they can revise their work and celebrate their learning and creations, which in

Paul Solarz

Mrs. Wideen

Linda Yollis

turn gives their skills and knowledge authenticity. Paul Solarz, Mrs. Wideen, and Linda Yollis are three strong examples of educators who have harnessed the power of social media to share their students' work and engage them in the power of technology as a tool for learning.

Let's end by taking a quick look at the role of digital portfolios. (See Appendix 4.) As your students begin to create and document their learning in different ways, they need a place to house their creations so that they are both easily accessible to them (curate), but also easily accessible to a wide audience (connect). Your students should be the ones responsible for making the decisions about which creations they want to share in their portfolios. They may want to share the creations they are in the process of developing. They may want to share creations they have completed, and there may be times when they want to remove an item after it has been shared for a while. The role of curating their portfolio should be theirs; we want to give them ownership of their learning. Their digital portfolio gives them voice and pride because they have something that they want to share with the world.

5

The Role of Questioning

For students to become lifelong learners, they need to be questioners and risk-takers! As such, questioning must become an essential strategy educators employ. Educators' ability to ask open-ended, engaging questions of students is invaluable and will transform learning and assessment in daily practice. While questioning plays a role in all three types of assessment, asking open–ended and thought-provoking questions is especially essential for assessment *as* learning.

Most educators would agree that we have a propensity to help students. While this seems positive, our tendency is to respond to students' questions with direct and closed answers, resulting in learners who are less likely to explore, challenge themselves, and develop their curiosity. In order to reverse this, we need to respond to their questions with encouraging comments and challenging, guiding questions.

We need to encourage students to explore and engage their curiosity and to provide them with the opportunities and the means to create authentic demonstrations of their learning.

> *Learners should be able to construct meaning for themselves, reflect on the significance of the meaning, and self-assess to determine their own strengths and weaknesses. Integrated curricula, cooperative learning, and problem-based learning are just a few examples of curricula that help students construct knowledge for themselves.*

Ken O'Connor

A More
Beautiful
Question

Warren Berger, in his thought-provoking book, *A More Beautiful Question*, discusses the role of questioning in the business world and in education. He believes the reason schools don't teach or encourage questions is that questions challenge authority and disrupt established structures, processes, and systems—forcing people to have to at least think about doing something different.

When I give educators a challenge to work on during my workshops, I have noticed that they want me to tell them what their answers should be. For example, when I asked participants to examine the differences between digitized learning and creating digital learning experiences for their students and to create an example of both, they asked me for an example of digital learning. They were visibly thrown out of their comfort zone when I responded with a guiding question and encouragement rather than with a direct answer. When I asked why they wanted me to give them the answer instead of using their curiosity and imagination, through reflection they admitted that when they were students, their teachers responded to them in a closed manner, which discouraged them from asking questions. They had learned to ask a question, receive an answer, and give the teacher what they wanted in order to get a good mark. This was learned behavior that discouraged original thought. This realization reflected an *aha* moment for many of the participants. Educators must be cognizant of the impact of closed responses on learners and keep questioning at the forefront of planning and responding.

At the end of this workshop, I asked the participants to use Padlet to reflect anonymously on their learning, which allowed those who otherwise may have been reluctant to be frank and share. The feedback was extremely informative to me as assessment *for* learning and assessment *as* learning. I now have evidence of their learning to use as I plan Part Two of the workshop (Figure 5-1).

The Padlet is an excellent example of assessment as learning and demonstrates the importance of teacher reflection. Reflection on our practices is the only way to improve them and develop teaching and learning opportunities for students using technology as a tool. Without reflective practice, there is no openness or understanding of the need to continually improve how we engage and help students learn.

"Reflective practice is a dialogue of thinking and doing through which I become more skillful."
—Donald A. Schön, *The Reflective Practitioner*

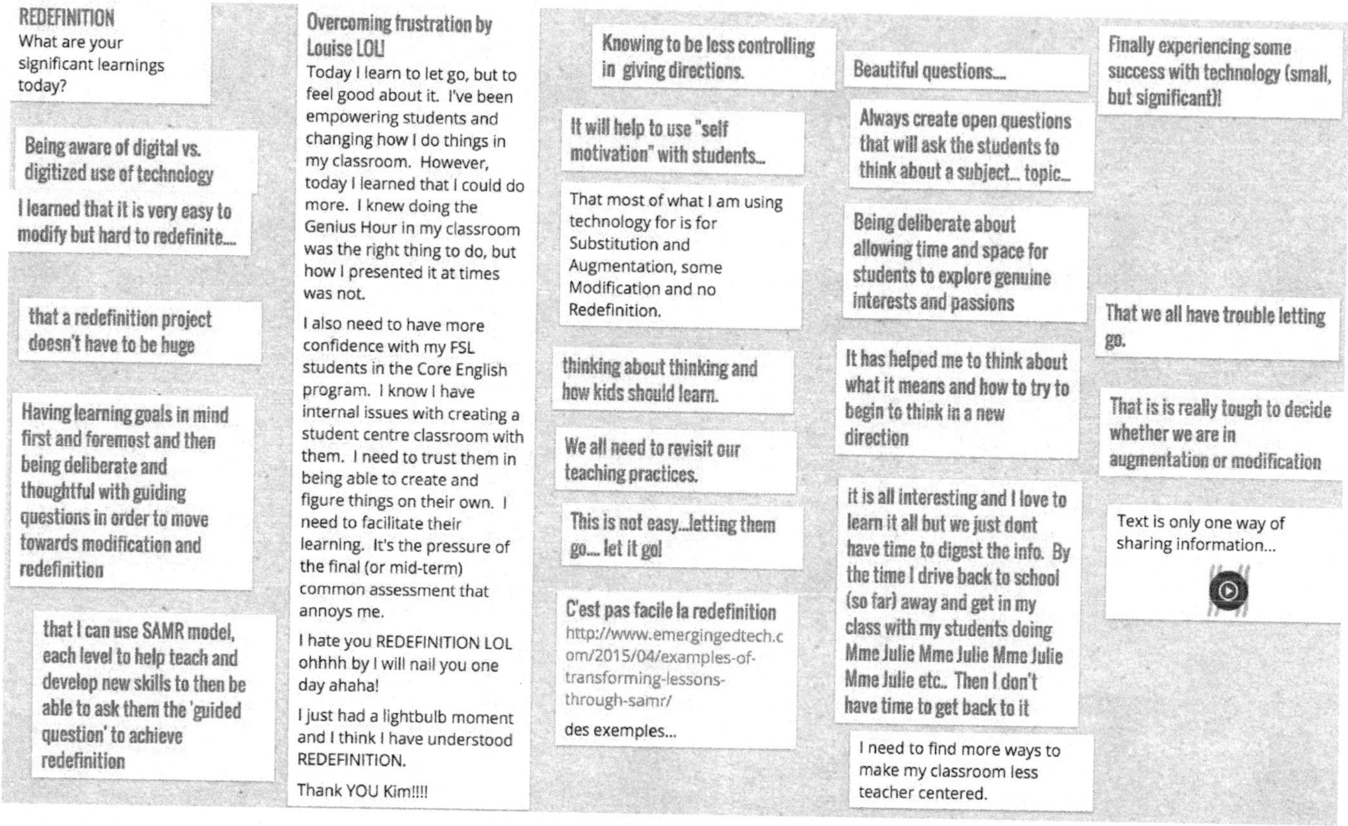

REDEFINITION
What are your significant learnings today?

Being aware of digital vs. digitized use of technology

I learned that it is very easy to modify but hard to redefinite...

that a redefinition project doesn't have to be huge

Having learning goals in mind first and foremost and then being deliberate and thoughtful with guiding questions in order to move towards modification and redefinition

that I can use SAMR model, each level to help teach and develop new skills to then be able to ask them the guided question to achieve redefinition

Overcoming frustration by Louise LOL!
Today I learn to let go, but to feel good about it. I've been empowering students and changing how I do things in my classroom. However, today I learned that I could do more. I knew doing the Genius Hour in my classroom was the right thing to do, but how I presented it at times was not.

I also need to have more confidence with my FSL students in the Core English program. I know I have internal issues with creating a student centre classroom with them. I need to trust them in being able to create and figure things on their own. I need to facilitate their learning. It's the pressure of the final (or mid-term) common assessment that annoys me.

I hate you REDEFINITION LOL ohhhh by I will nail you one day ahaha!

I just had a lightbulb moment and I think I have understood REDEFINITION.

Thank YOU Kim!!!!

Knowing to be less controlling in giving directions.

It will help to use "self motivation" with students...

That most of what I am using technology for is for Substitution and Augmentation, some Modification and no Redefinition.

thinking about thinking and how kids should learn.

We all need to revisit our teaching practices.

This is not easy...letting them go... let it go!

C'est pas facile la redefinition http://www.emergingedtech.com/2015/04/examples-of-transforming-lessons-through-samr/ des exemples...

Beautiful questions...

Always create open questions that will ask the students to think about a subject.. topic...

Being deliberate about allowing time and space for students to explore genuine interests and passions

It has helped me to think about what it means and how to try to begin to think in a new direction

it is all interesting and I love to learn it all but we just dont have time to digest the info. By the time I drive back to school (so far) away and get in my class with my students doing Mme Julie Mme Julie Mme Julie Mme Julie etc. Then I don't have time to get back to it

I need to find more ways to make my classroom less teacher centered.

Finally experiencing some success with technology (small, but significant!)

That is is really tough to decide whether we are in augmentation or modification

That we all have trouble letting go.

Text is only one way of sharing information...

Figure 5-1

6

Assessment OF Learning

Assessment *of* learning should consist of rich information gathered over a period of time through assessment *as* learning and assessment *for* learning. However, too often that is not the case. As such, assessment *of* learning was by far the most difficult chapter to write. I avoided it. I even told my friends that I wanted to omit it altogether! Assessment *of* learning is the time when we have to look at the rich information we have gathered about the learning of our students and transform it into marks to report to parents. Unfortunately, as soon as we do this and communicate it with a few comments (usually from a pre-created bank), the richness of the information we have about how our students are learning is diminished.

All aspects of assessment have the potential to be subjective, but too often the perception is that assessment *of* learning is less subjective

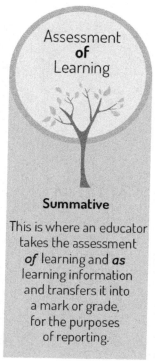

Assessment of Learning

Summative

This is where an educator takes the assessment *of* learning and *as* learning information and transfers it into a mark or grade, for the purposes of reporting.

than assessment *as* and *for* learning. This cannot be further from the truth. If educators have strong knowledge of the developmental continuum of learning, then the level of subjectivity is greatly reduced. It is the progress of a student's learning that must be communicated to parents. The rich assessment information documented through student creations (which students can curate in their digital portfolio) will allow the teacher and the student to articulate growth and skill development. It will also provide evidence to support their mark.

Educators must plan all teaching and learning opportunities, whether traditional methods or those using technology, based on learning goals. Educators must begin with the curriculum expectations and share with their students the skills and knowledge they need to demonstrate. Although educators may plan teaching and learning opportunities based on the curriculum, when it comes to assessment *of* learning, they often use their personal judgments to determine the mark. Instead of basing marks on assessment information gathered, educators often measure students against fellow classmates, against their personal opinions about where a student's learning should be, and/or based on paper-and-pencil tests rather than on the assessment information gathered. Even educators who provide students with rich learning opportunities may not be confident in their assessment skills and opt to give a mark based on a paper-and-pencil test.

Unfortunately, a paper-and-pencil test, by nature of its design, cannot reflect true student learning. From the strategies provided in previous chapters, it should be evident that assessment *of* learning information can be gathered through the student's creation and diverse demonstrations of their learning using technology as a tool.

High Tech High

I recognize that taking all of the rich assessment information gathered through the process and product of creation and then assigning a mark is difficult. In an ideal world, we would be sharing our students' work with their parents, articulating their successes, addressing their challenges, and setting realistic goals for their continued growth—and not concerning ourselves with quantifying a student's development. I love the way that a high school in San Diego, High Tech High, has their students create and present their work to an audience of parents and professionals in the field. Talk about making thinking visible and making learning authentic!

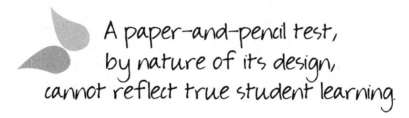

A paper-and-pencil test, by nature of its design, cannot reflect true student learning.

It is difficult to provide specific advice on assessment *of* learning because each school district/board and independent school has its own parameters for grading students, but there are some examples of "best practice" that can be reflected upon. One of the practices that warrants discussion is the use of rubrics, guides listing specific criteria for grading.

Rubrics can be extremely helpful to educators making summative assessment decisions, but unfortunately, their decisions are only as good as the rubric itself. The Ontario Ministry of Education has excellent examples of strong rubrics and

Ontario Ministry of Education

exemplars. A strong rubric must include detailed information about the criteria being assessed and needs to be paired with exemplars, which are examples drawn from different students' work that demonstrate the progression of learning. Without exemplars, the measure of a student's creation against the rubric is almost always based on the teacher's judgment. The challenge this presents is that an A assigned by one teacher in grade ten geography can look very different from an A assigned in the grade ten geography class next door.

Based on best practices in assessment *of* learning, summative decisions must involve the use of rich assessment information gathered from students' creations using technology as a tool. Technology as a tool for learning provides rich documentation to support the summative grade and serves as evidence of student learning to be shared at parent-teacher conferences—evidence which is much richer than any gathered from a paper-and-pencil assignment or test.

Tracy Zordan shared the following examples of summative assessment using technology as a tool for learning in her science class. In place of a traditional test for the lymphatic and immune systems and vaccines unit, she allowed students to choose any format they wanted to demonstrate their learning and understanding. Not surprisingly, many chose to use digital tools. Students received a list of topics to be covered and spent class time discussing many different possibilities for projects, which included a Minecraft tour and a Lego stop-motion animation. The use of technology provided students a forum to spend quality time with the subject matter, which, in turn, allowed for a deeper level of learning and retention. Also, students were able to keep these artifacts more easily as evidence of their learning progress. In addition, Tracy asked each student to write on a Google Form the three criteria they felt were important for evaluation, which they then shared with the class. From the ensuing discussion, Tracy was able to create a meaningful rubric for the project.

When Tracy's class conducted an eye dissection lab, she provided a list of structures students needed to identify during the lab. Some students chose to turn in a digital format to demonstrate their learning. During a lab, it is difficult for the teacher to circulate to evaluate each student's ability to identify the structures. A digital demonstration of their work allowed Tracy more time for evaluation and, more importantly, provided her with greater understanding of her students' progression of learning.

Tracy's examples and reflection validate the idea that, by allowing students to demonstrate their learning in different ways, an educator can meet summative evaluation requirements while gathering incredible information about how the student is learning. Think of assessment *of* learning not solely as a means for grading but more importantly as a means of communicating student learning. Your main role as an educator, with respect to assessment *for*, *as*, and *of* learning, is to use the rich assessment information you gather from your students' creations to provide them with the guidance, encouragement, and direct instruction they need to become curious and innovative lifelong learners!

Conclusion

We cannot deny technology plays an integral role in the lives of our students and will continue to do so in inconceivable ways. As educators, we must harness the power that technology as a tool for learning has to contribute to the development of skilled lifelong learners. It is our responsibility to help our students develop their ability to access information and determine fact from fiction (consume) as well as guide students to transform their knowledge into coherent and innovative demonstrations of learning (create). Students also need us to help them filter information (consume), assimilate it with prior knowledge, and responsibly share it with others (connect and curate).

By using technology as a tool for learning, students can develop their literacy skills, their factual knowledge, their creativity, and their digital legacy. This is why educators must have strong skills in assessing their students' demonstrations of learning using diverse means and mediums. The assessment information gathered must be the means by which guiding questions are formed, direct instruction is determined, feedback and encouragement are created, and new learning opportunities are planned.

As you read this book, you have had the opportunity to explore a variety of strategies and examples of how students can demonstrate their learning using technology as a tool. You have seen how these demonstrations provide rich assessment information. You have engaged your metacognition, visualizing and reflecting on how to transform your teaching practices to inspire lifelong learning. I encourage you to discuss with your PLN what in this book has resonated with you and reflect on your current practices with the aim of making some potentially difficult decisions. As you reflect, consider these vital questions:

- What practices can you celebrate and continue?
- Are there practices you need to abandon?
- What new practices do you need to embrace?
- Are you creating teaching and learning opportunities for your students to demonstrate their learning using technology?
- Are you encouraging and guiding your students based on their passions, personal skills, and prior knowledge?

I asked Jaime Casap, Google Global Education Evangelist, "What does technology mean to you?" I was delighted by his response and share it with you, as it is the perfect conclusion to the journey you and I have just taken together:

James Casap

I think we've been talking about technology as a tool for a very long time. Motion pictures were a tool. Televisions were a tool. Computers have been a tool since the sixties. Today we include computers, tablets, applications, websites, etc. when we define technology. When we wrap up all those elements together, what it means to me is that we are at a point where these tools are getting easy to use, easy to manage, easy to scale. These are the greatest tools we have ever had to support and enable great teaching and learning, as long as we always keep in mind that they are only as powerful as we want them to be. On their own they have no value, but as an enabling and supporting capability, they are the most powerful tools we have ever had!

The world is at our fingertips.
Is the world available to your students?

Acknowledgments

In a world of rapidly changing information and ever-evolving technological tools that have the capacity to improve student learning, it is a blessing to have a strong professional learning network (PLN). I would not have thought about writing this book, let alone completing it, without my PLN.

I would like to thank Michael Chechile for his vision and support. He was the Director of Educational Services at the Lester B. Pearson School Board for the first few years of my involvement in technology as a tool for learning and is now the Director General. He has a powerful vision of what learning must look like for Generation Z and has been integral in the gradual transformation of our school district to become Future Ready. His trust and support has allowed me to grow as an educator and have opportunities to learn outside my work context.

Special thanks to my friend and colleague, Tanya Avrith—who recognizes my passion for teaching and learning and my understanding of technology—for inviting me with open arms into the journey you had started at our district to begin using Google Apps for Education. It is invaluable to have a like-minded person with an incredible growth mindset to help develop ideas and challenge me to do my best. Our daily chats and sharing ideas for workshops we were planning made my writing possible. How wonderful to have a pedagogical soulmate!

To my colleague, Antonio Fuoco, thank you for all of your support and partnership. It is invaluable to have such amazing teamwork between an IT consultant and a pedagogical consultant. You have taught me about the technological aspects needed to make technology as a tool for learning possible.

One of the biggest challenges I faced when writing was wondering if my content made sense, was clear, and, of course, was of any interest. Thank goodness I had my editors, encouragers, and thought–provokers, Sam Bruzzese, Amira Rahman and James Petersen. Sam—the lifelong learner, retired Principal, Adjunct Professor, and passionate advocate for twenty-first-century learning—you made the completion of this book possible! Amira Rahman, thank you for your invaluable contributions through your detailed editing and clarifying questioning throughout my writing process. James Petersen. You are brilliant and humble and want the best for students! Your critical perspective and keen editing helped me immensely! It is always a pleasure working with the three of you!

Thank you, Julie Phenix for working so patiently with me to create graphics that represented my thoughts and words.

To the publishing team at EDTechTeam, thank you so much for the opportunity to share my passion for learning and the critical role of assessment. Thank you in particular to Holly Clark, Head of Publishing, who encouraged me to write this book and played an integral role in my ongoing involvement in the world of educational technology. Thanks also to Holly and Ken Shelton for giving me opportunities to present at EDTechTeam summits, where I continue to learn and share ideas with like-minded colleagues. Thank you both for all your support and encouragement.

In conclusion, I would like to thank my loving family for your immense support. Special thanks to my parents who are always available to take care of my aging dog so I can continue to learn new and exciting things!

Appendix 1

One Screen of Chrome Apps

Web Store

Google Docs

Google Drive

Google Slides

Google Sheets

Google Drawings

Snapverter

Voice Recorder

Kaizena (Voice Comme...

Read closely. Think cri...

YouTube

Drive Template Gallery

Pixlr Editor

Math Apps

Desmos Graphing Calc...

ThingLink

WeVideo - Video Edito...

TweetDeck by Twitter

Facebook

Classroom

Soundtrap

Padlet

Canva

Appendix 2

Steps to Create a Screencast Video for Reading Fluency

1. Open a Google Doc.

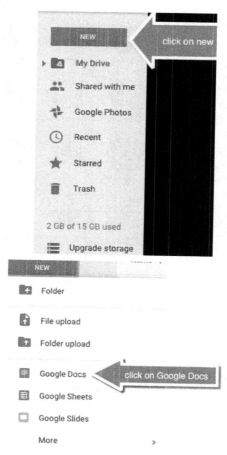

2. Copy and paste text selected at the student's reading level.

3. Instruct the student to launch Screencastify and then begin reading using the mouse/arrow to point to each word.

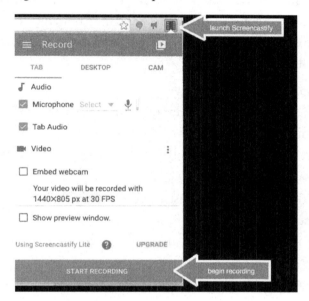

Appendix 3

Marshmallow Challenge

I introduce this activity during the first three days of the school year in my grade nine classes. Students are randomly placed in groups which I name after scientists I doubt the students know much about. The groups are mixed gender, and I do not know anything about the students' abilities.

Instructions and Rules

- Build the tallest freestanding structure, using only the materials provided.
- Materials include twenty pieces of spaghetti, one meter of tape, one meter of string, and one marshmallow.
- The final structure must be freestanding; it cannot be suspended.
- The ENTIRE marshmallow must be on top of the structure. Cutting or eating it disqualifies the team.
- Any amount of the provided materials can be used, but the bag holding the materials cannot be used.
- Spaghetti CAN be broken; tape and string can be cut.
- The structure CANNOT be touched or supported when it is measured.
- Each team has minutes to plan and build the structure.

Procedure

- Each student individually makes a sketch of his/her proposed design and puts his/her name on the back of the sketch.
- Then have a student take a picture of each person's design with the iPad.

- Each group discusses the sketches of each team member and chooses a design to construct. The decision can be a combination of multiple ideas.
- Record at least three reasons the group chose the design they chose.
- Build your structure.
- Each structure is measured at the end of the eighteen minutes.

Reporting

- Each group creates a report using Explain Everything.
- The report must contain:
- The group's name and all individuals' names
- The individual design proposals (pictures)
- The group's final design (picture)
- Three reasons for selecting the final design
- A picture of the structure being measured
- Testing results (height if the structure was standing)
- Change to improve your group's design

BONUS: Include a picture and/or information about the scientist for whom your team is named.

Appendix 4

Digital Portfolio: Process

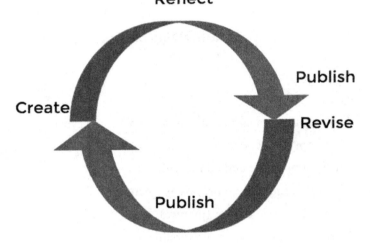

Reflect

Publish

Create

Revise

Publish

Workflow for Digital Portfolios

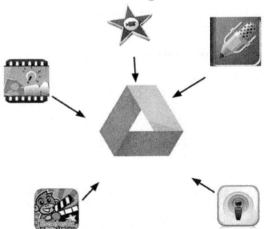

Workflow: Digital Portfolios Using Sites

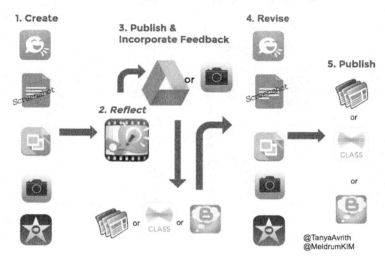

Digital Portfolio Process - Publishing

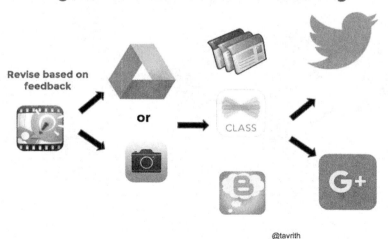

Workflow: Digital Portfolios Using Sites

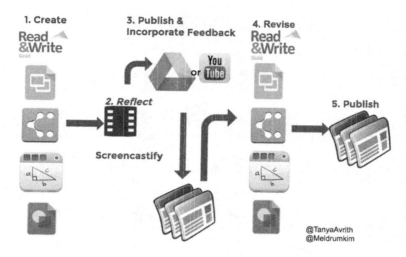

Digital Portfolio Process - Publishing

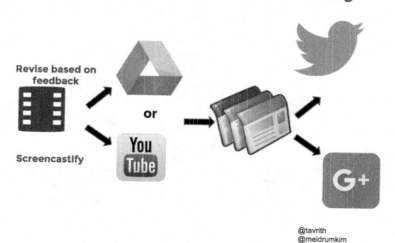

Digital Portfolio Process - Publishing

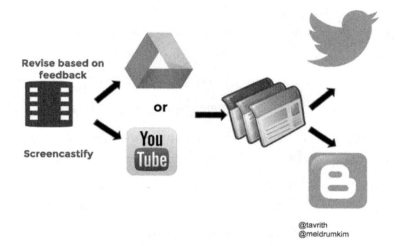

Works Cited

Merriam-Webster, 09 Feb. 2016,
http://www.merriam-webster.com/dictionary/assessment

"Adrian Conics," *YouTube,* 17 Feb. 2016,
https://www.youtube.com/watch?v=G_9rdCwuMPg

Avrith, Tanya, 09 Feb. 2016, http://www.tanyaavrith.com

Beattie, Bill, Goodreads Inc., 2016, https://www.goodreads.com/author/quotes/1911926.Bill_Beattie

Bruner, Jerome as cited in "My English Pages," Aug, 2011, http://www.myenglishpages.com/blog/jerome-bruners-constructivist-theory

Caisap, Jaime, *Education Evangelist,* 2016,
http://www.jcasap.com/

Clark, Tim, *BYOT Network,* 09 Feb. 2016,
https://byotnetwork.com

Dwerk, Carol, *Mindset,* 09 Feb. 2016, http://mindsetonline.com/whatisit/about/

EdTechTeam, 11 Feb. 2016, https://www.edtechteam.com

"Explain Everything Interactive Whiteboard," *Explain Everything,* 20 Feb. 2016, http://explaineverthing.com

Freebody & Luke's "Four Resources Model", (1990), *Literacy for the Twenty-First Century,* Ontario Education Secretariat, 2004.

Fullan, Michael, *Stratosphere: Integrating Technology, Pedagogy, and Change Knowledge,* Pearson, 2012.

"Growing Success: Assessment and Evaluation in Ontario's Schools," *Ontario Ministry of Education*, 2010, http://www.edu.gov. on.ca/eng/policyfunding/growSuccess.pdf

Hattie, John, *Visible Learning for Teachers: Maximizing Impact on Learning*, Routledge, 2012.

International Society of Technology in Education, 2016, http:// www.iste.org/standards/ISTE-standards/standards-for-coaches

Kleon, Austin, *Show Your Work!: 10 Ways to Share Your Creativity and Get Discovered*, Workman Publishing Company, 2014.

McCrindle, Mark, *Generation Z*, http://generationz.com.au/ learning-styles/

O'Connor, Ken, "Ken O'Connor, Education Consultant, The Grade Doctor," 09 Feb. 2016, oconnorgrading.com

The Ontario Curriculum–Exemplars Grades 1-8, Queen's Printer for Ontario, 1999.

Pan, Maria, https://twitter.com/mspan100

Preston, Jane, https://twitter.com/jane_preston66

Puentedura, Ruben R. Dr., *Hippasus*, 09 Feb. 2016, http://www. hippasus.com

"Resources and Downloads to Facilitate Inquiry-Based Learning," *Edutopia*, http://www.edutopia.org/article/ inquiry-based-learning-resources-downloads#graph2

Roskos, Tabors, & Lenhart, 2005. P.V. Eisenhart, Corinne, "Mss. Reading First Conference," August, 2008

Petersen, James, *Open Source Teacher*, 09 Feb. 2016, *http://www. opensourceteacher.ca*

"Reflective Teaching: Exploring Our Own Classroom Practice," British Council, 2012, http://www.teachingenglish.org.uk/article/reflective-teaching-exploring-our-own-classroom-practice

Ritchhart, Ron, Mark Church, and Karin Morrison, *Making Thinking Visible: How to Promote Engagement, Understanding, and Independence for All Learners,* Jossey-Bass, 2011.

Roskos, Kathy, Patton O. Tabors, and Lisa A. Lenhart, *Oral Language and Early Literacy in Preschool: Talking,* Reading, and Writing, International Reading Association, 2004.

Schön, Donald A., *The Reflective Practitioner: How Professionals Think in Action,* Basic Books Inc., 1983.

Shelton, Kenneth, Inspire Motive Educate Create, 09 Feb. 2016, http://kennethshelton.net/

Solarz, Paul, *What Is Going on In Mr. Solarz's Class,* http://psolarz.weebly.com/mr-solarz-eportfolio

"Teaching English, British Council, BBC." *TeachingEnglish,* 09 Feb. 2016, teachingenglish.org.uk.

"Transform Teaching and Learning," International Society for Technology in Education, 09 Feb. 2016, http://www.iste.org

"Using Explain Everything in the Primary Classroom," *Mrs. Wideen's Blog,* 17 Feb. 2016, http://www.mrswideen.com

Wagner, Tony, and Robert A. Compton, *Creating Innovators: The Making of Young People Who Will Change the World,* Scribner, 2012.

Yollis, Linda, *Mrs. Yollis's Classroom Blog,* 2016, http://yollisclassblog.blogspot.ca/

Zordan, Tracy, https://twitter.com/tracyzordan

About the Author

KIM MELDRUM, M.ED. is a passionate educator, presenter, and author. Focused on using technology to support good pedagogical practice, Kim works to change the way educators view digital tools and has presented at educational technology conferences including ISTE 2015, ASCD (2015), the first Canadian Google for Education Leadership Symposium, and EdTechTeam Google for Education Summits.

Kim's expertise includes a focus on effective differentiation, digital literacies, assessment, and reflective learning practice. She was instrumental in the successful adoption and support of Google Apps for Education at the Lester B. Pearson School Board in Montreal, Quebec. Kim also has responsibilities in the implementation of her school district's widely respected Digital Citizenship Program. In 2015, the Lester B. Pearson School Board's digital citizenship journey was highlighted in Mike Ribble's *Digital Citizenship in Schools Third Edition*.

Kim is a device-agnostic educator who encourages education professionals (including teachers and administrators) to develop a growth mindset and take risks in the classroom in order to transform teaching and learning for students.

kimmeldrum.com
@meldrumkim

CPSIA information can be obtained
at www.ICGtesting.com
Printed in the USA
FSOW03n1350170616
21681FS